The Center for Western Studies is a cultural museum and a study and research agency of Augustana College, Sioux Falls, South Dakota, concerned principally with South Dakota and the adjoining states, the Prairie Plains, and with certain aspects of the Great Plains and the Trans-Mississippi West.

The Center serves as a resource for teachers, research scholars, students and the general public, through which studies, research projects and related activities are initiated and conducted, and by which assistance can be provided to interested individuals and groups. Its goal is to provide awareness of the multi-faceted culture of this area, with special emphasis on Dakota (Sioux) Indian Culture.

The Center was founded in the conviction that this region possesses a unique and important heritage which should not be lost or forgotten. Consequently, the Center for Western Studies seeks to provide services to assist researchers in their study of the region, to promote a public consciousness of the importance of preserving cultural and historical resources, to collect published and unpublished materials, art and artifacts, important to the understanding of the region, and to undertake and sponsor projects, to sponsor conferences and provide permanent displays and shows which reflect the art and culture of the West, particularly the Sioux.

The Center maintains an archive and possesses one of the finest collections available of books relating to all aspects of the American West. The Center continually seeks to expand its collections in order to provide maximum assistance to interested scholars, students at all levels, and the general public. The collections include excellent representative Sioux Indian art, bead and quill work, western art consisting of original oils, water colors, bronzes, photographs, and steel engravings.

FREDERICK MANFRED:
A Bibliography and Publishing History

Rodney J. Mulder

Department of Sociology
Grand Valley State College
Allendale, MI 49401

John H. Timmerman

Department of English
Calvin College
Grand Rapids, MI 49506

Published by
THE CENTER FOR WESTERN STUDIES
AN
HISTORICAL RESEARCH AND ARCHIVAL
Agency of
Augustana College
Sioux Falls,
South Dakota

ISBN: Number 0-931170-15-X
Library of Congress Catalog Number 81-67077
ALL RIGHTS RESERVED
Copyright 1981 by the Center for Western Studies
First Edition
Printed by Crescent Publishing Company, Hills, Minnesota
Manufactured in the United States of America

FREDERICK MANFRED

ACKNOWLEDMENTS

Special thanks are due three gentlemen without whose help this project could not have been completed. Frederick Manfred has been gracious with his time, his files, his stories, and his good humor. He has been interrogated like a suspect in major crime when his only crime has been to craft his art. For his art and his patience, our thanks. Alan Lathrop, librarian at the University of Minnesota and organizer of the Manfred Collection, similarly had his patience tried under our excavation of many boxes of notes, letters, and manuscripts. It was archaeology on a still living site. Also, we thank Sven Froiland, whose enthusiasm for this project has made the labor a pleasure and who has endured a barrage of last minute changes and refinements with grace.

The editors and scholars who have assisted this project by correspondence and telephone are too numerous to list, but we remember them collectively with appreciation.

This space permits the rare pleasure of more personal acknowledgment as well, and we take the opportunity to thank our wives Lucarol and Patricia, and our parents, long time friends of Manfred.

Table of Contents

Introduction... 10
Section A: Original Books............................. 15
Section B: Other Works................................ 77
Section C: Critical Studies of Manfred's Work
    I. Critical Articles and Books, Annotated............ 85
    II. Checklist of News Reports and Miscellaneous Items.. 92
    III. Dissertations and Theses....................... 97
Section D: Book Reviews............................... 99
Narrative Interview................................... 119

Introduction

In one of the earliest critical assessments of Manfred's work, John R. Milton concluded his essay by stating of the author: "He is well on his way to becoming a major American author."[1] This was in 1957 and was based on the novelist's first eight works. Since then the output of books has tripled to twenty-four; the books have served as basis for serious and thorough critical investigation, and (to cite that indisputable yardstick) several thousand pages of graduate theses and dissertations have been written, considered, and approved. Yet in that same early essay with its optimistic prophecy, Milton hints at a reality which has not changed greatly, the disaffection of the eastern literary establishment with the western novelist. Indeed, Milton spent the first six or seven paragraphs of his essay accounting for this fact. Much more could be written.

It remains, then, an interesting speculation: the place of the western writer in American letters. The curious fact remains that while novelists like Manfred, Vardis Fisher, A.B. Guthrie, Jr., Walter Van Tilburg Clark, and others are commonly mentioned as "major" American writers, and while they have survived well the critical scrutiny of academic insight, their popular acclaim, with few exceptions, has remained uncommonly small. Few of their works reside for more than a brief spell on the best seller lists--and when they do, they appear there as a strange cousin who slipped in a back door and crashed the party. Related but not a member of the family. Manfred has had two books, This is the Year and Lord Grizzly, on the national best seller list, and those briefly.

Classic, enduring literature is not determined of course by best seller lists. When Thoreau's A Week on the Concord and Merrimack Rivers sold a scant 219 copies in five years of his self-paid, 1,000 copy run, the author remarked with grim humor: "I have now a library of nearly nine hundred volumes, over seven hundred of which I wrote myself." The back of that volume boldly announced that Walden was forthcoming. It coming forth was belated; but it sold better, 2,000 copies in seven years.

There was little promise then that Walden would be a classic, that copies of the work would be issued by the thousands and not

---

[1] John R. Milton, "Voice from Siouxland: Frederick Feikema Manfred," College English, XIX (Dec, 1957), p. 111.

only issued but read. It is not the task of this bibliography to hazard a prophetic statement on Manfred's place in future generations, but on the basis of critical studies included in this bibliography it may be safe to suggest that several of his works are in fact classics. A classic should, at the least, possess the following traits: 1) Aesthetic excellence--it must be a work of fine art. 2) Universality of meaning and significance--it applies to peoples of different times and places. 3) Anchorage in history and a life experience--it must have something significant to say about the time in which it is written or about which it is written. 4) Spiritual significance--it must be revealing of man's quest for human and spiritual meaning. Those are but a few primary traits in what could be a lengthy list. Several of Manfred's major works bear clear evidence of such traits.

We are left, then, with the curious question of why such works should be studiously ignored by the literary marketplace of the eastern publishing world. There may be reasons, of course, that are inherent in Manfred's novels. For example, one can point to certain stylistic oddities in the early novels. The reviewers of these novels pointed out an adequate number of such peculiarities and they need not be recounted here. But the point has lost its force. Manfred's style has evolved into a smooth and graceful flow, marked by startling skill in imagery, dialogue, and evocation of place. Another reason, however, may well be a deep-rooted prejudice by the eastern literary establishment to the regional flavor of the novels. The publishing world, for the most part, has been lukewarm to regionalists in our century, and has been slow to recognize that in the particular one might see more clearly the universal significance. "Siouxland" has an odd ring to it. Something like Yoknapatawpha.

The publishing world has been guilty of negligence in recognizing the peculiar spirit of this art. Western literature is often mythic in the sense in which Mircea Eliade uses the term in his Myth and Reality.[2] Such literature begins in the physical thing in order to seek the primordial thing; the real meaning behind the fact. The work tells a story in one place in time in order to better understand the story which caused that place in time. Ill at ease with the physical thing and the present story, some have failed to recognize the larger scope and spirit of western art. Max West-

---

[2] Mircea Eliade, Myth and Reality (New York: Harper and Row, 1963).

brook has provided one of the better accountings of this in his essay "Conservative, Liberal, and Western: Three Modes of American Realism," in which he argues that "in Eastern realism the conscious mind is primary: in Western realism the unconscious mind is primary."[3] The sense of the western mind is oriented around the primordial as Mircea Eliade uses that term. In the east we have an orientation which may be described as Emerson did in "The American Scholar;" that is, Man Thinking. The eastern mind is analytic; the western speculative, open-ended. The result of these different orientations, Westbrook concludes, is this: "Emphasis on the conscious mind causes the Easterner to be discontent with what strikes him as an irresponsible structure in much of Western art."[4] If that structure seems irresponsible, or open-ended at times, it is to provide room for the searching, outward directed mind.

While Manfred has been accused of precisely this transgression by eastern reviewers and publishers, it must be admitted that Manfred has gotten in his own shots at the eastern literary establishment. They have been good shots. One of the more carefully worded public statements appears in "The Novelists of Western America," which concludes with this tongue in cheek (and clenched teeth) statement: "So we starve as we write, and our children wear hand-me-downs, and our wives go mad looking through wish-books while lying in bed under a pile of buffalo robes in a cold house."[5]

All this may not seem very important except to bibliographers who have a perverse interest in such matters and authors who would like to put food on the family table. But in Manfred's instance the issue has artistic significance. Early on, the genius of the man's writings attracted a potentially wide press. He determined, nonetheless, that he was going to craft his own peculiar vision by his artistic means. The opportunity for the big dollar has been available more than once, but the opportunity sometimes

---

[3]Max Westbrook, "Conservative, Liberal, and Western: Three Modes of American Realism," The South Dakota Review, IV (Summer, 1966), p. 14.

[4]Ibid.

[5]Frederick Manfred, "The Novelists of Western America," Chicago Daily News (January 7, 1967), Panorama Section, p. 8.

stood at odds with his particular artistic voice and vision. The bibliographic history of Manfred is not only, then, a story of who sold or bought what; but it is also the story of the pursuance of an artistic vision.

The goal of this bibliography is to provide as full a description as possible of Manfred's literary production, and also to chronicle a remarkable story of a western author in the contemporary publishing world. One quickly recognizes that Manfred's readers have been devoted readers, and collections of his works have become prized possessions among them.[6] As a result of this avid readership, literally dozens of press interviews have been written in areas of large readership--primarily in the Siouxland area of Minnesota, South Dakota, and Iowa, and also in the Great Lakes Midwest. Gradually his work has gained a larger critical audience in academic circles. The Western Literature Association's 1977 Conference devoted a large portion of their agenda to Manfred studies, and the collection of essays that evolved from that Conference, Where the West Begins, reflected this in its selection of essays on Manfred.

The guiding principle in this study is to describe Manfred's literary corpus and the related scholarship, but also to reconstruct a publishing history for that corpus. This principle necessarily affects method. Therefore, detailed notes on bibliographic method will precede major sections of this study. We have given the novelist the last word by including the narrative interview at the conclusion of this study.

---

[6]One method of determining the degree of reader interest is through used book dealers who cater to the whims and demands of collectors. By late 1980 certain works were commanding princely prices. Individual volumes of the early World's Wanderer Trilogy, which in 1975 were still being sold for $3.00-$5.00, were listed for a minimum of $20.00. Arrow of Love, when it can be found, goes for $150.00-$200.00. Winter Count in the first edition is a bargain at $30.00. First editions of the Buckskin Man Series range up to $40.00. As recently as 1978 a dealer who bought and retailed Alan Swallow's stock after Swallow's death sold Morning Red and Wanderlust at list price. A year later the volumes were in demand at prices ranging to $50.00 and $100.00 respectively.

Section A: Original Books

While Manfred's professional career as a novelist dates from the publication of The Golden Bowl in 1944, considerable writing activity preceded this. His college publications are listed in this bibliography in order to reveal some of this activity. Other works are not a part of public record. For example, an aborted effort entitled "Millions of Morons" written in 1934 amounted to 101 pages of manuscript. One will also find in the Manfred Archives at the University of Minnesota a One Act Play of 96 pages entitled "Give Us This Day" that dates from the late thirties. Two folders in the Archives, one dated 1928-1929, the other 1933-1936, are stuffed with unpublished short stories. Some of the titles of these pieces reflect the novelistic bent of mind already developing: "A Western Sale on a Farm" (1933) which contains some similarities to the auction in This is the Year, "Thoughts in a Hay Loft" (1935), "Another Furrow" (1936), "Sunlight on the Golden Fuzz" (1940).

Some of these early works were to see fruition in later years. Sections of Green Earth, for example, actually date back to Manfred's college notebooks. A manuscript given the working title of "A Time to Remember" in the late thirties and early forties contained the germ of Sons of Adam, published by Crown in 1980. In this case the germ was nearly obliterated. An 800 page draft of "A Time to Remember," was burned by Manfred in the early forties. Only two actual pages from the manuscript (pages 83 and 117) survived and found their way into Sons of Adam. Two unpublished manuscripts, "The Rape of Elizabeth" and "The Mountain of Myrrh," were ravished and recast in Morning Red.

In addition to Sons of Adam, several other works are scheduled for publication or reprinting after the cut-off date for this bibliography (January 1, 1981). These include a book under the working title Prime Fathers. The work will contain long portraits of Manfred's father, Marlon Brando, Sinclair Lewis, and Hubert Humphrey. Briefer portraits of Frank Waters, Henry Miller, Max Eastman, Robert Penn Warren, and an essay "The Artist as the True Child of God" will also be included in the work. Gregg Press, a subsidiary of G.K. Hall, plans a series of reprints in hardcover which will include the Buckskin Man Series.

The primary effort in method in this section on Original Books is to describe the first edition of an original work as fully as possible so that it may be immediately identified by scholar or collector. Because of the concern for publishing history, later impressions, including paperback editions of the text, have been described more fully than is customary in bibliographic studies. Traditionally, these texts have been entered only by means of a checklist. In this instance, however, they further round out the publishing history we wish to detail. Further, our assumption here is that the paperback trade is an important phenomenon in twentieth century publishing and often represents a reader's first acquaintance with an author. Specific principles governing format and method are as follows.

1) Edition:

It may well be the case, as John Carter points out in his valuable little book ABC for Book Collectors, that modern emphasis upon the first edition is both somewhat misguided and something of a fetish. [1] Until the twentieth century book collectors were more concerned with the finest looking or best edited text. Mechanical production and the mass market in our time have largely flattened this curiousity for best-looking edition, and editing of a text has retained importance only in minor matters. In the case of Manfred, that editing does come to bear in certain instances, and these will be considered in the notes to Original Book entries.

In its simplest definition an edition is the number of copies of a book printed at any time or times from one setting-up of type. Increasingly, publishers identify the so-called "First Edition" as such somewhere in the front matter of the book. Hence, in the book descriptions we will supply such identification where and when it occurs and further distinguish between impressions (or copy runs of the type set-up at any one time).

The primary entry for the first edition of each Original Book will consist of the following:

A) Transcription of title page: This will distinguish between upper and lower case type but not in face design such as script or gothic or bold-face.

---

[1] John Carter, ABC for Book-Collectors (London: Rupert Hart-Davis, 1952).

B) Collation: This entry distinguishes in order the size of the leaf in centimeters, number of leaves, and pagination.
C) Contents: The entry here further identifies the edition according to front matter, dedication, prefaces, acknowledgments, epigraph quotations, and publisher's matter of importance.
D) Location in text of edition or impression identification.
E) Cover description: The entry here indicates design and color of cover. Little uniformity exists in describing colors of cloth used in publisher's bindings. Generally, fine degrees of discrimination are not particularly important in bibliographic studies of modern books. The effort here is to use vernacular terms (i.e., "light green") rather than using more esoteric idiom in order to readily identify the work.

2) RELATED DESCRIPTIONS:

In addition to standard bibliographic entries identifying the edition, included here are several items either of interest to the collector or of importance to the publishing history.
A) Dust Jacket: Purists among book collectors have had a general abhorrence of dust jackets, or "wrappers" as they have often been called. Like a paper bag, the "wrapper" was a delivery package intended to be disposed of. It is true that although the earliest recorded dust jacket dates back to 1832, until approximately World War I it was little more than a wrapper. Since that time the dust jacket has become a valued part of the book's total composition, so much so that a jacketed copy generally commands a considerably higher price on the collector's market. But the jacket has gained value for other reasons than collector's interest. The dust jacket often has inherent artistic interest and may be commissioned by an artist other than a house artist. For example, consider the Evelyn Raymond bust of Manfred which is depicted on the dust jackets of The Primitive, The Giant, and The Brother. Furthermore, the jacket often provides publishing information of some value, not the least of which is the often readily accessible price of the book located usually on the front flap of the jacket. Partly for these legitimate bibliographic interests, and partly for collector's curiousity, we have provided descriptive entries which identify the dust jacket of the first edition.
B) Place of Composition: Listed here are the place and approximate date of final composition. In some cases these are entered by Manfred on the final page of the text, an irregular practice he

adopted first in The Primitive. In that book and the other two of the World's Wanderer Trilogy the place entered is called Long Look, the first name for the Manfred home in Bloomington, Minnesota. How Long Look came to be called Wrâlda was related by Manfred thus:

> We never liked the name Long Look. One day, while in Bloomington, Little Freya [Manfred's daughter] heard our well pump working in the basement. She listened, and asked what that was. I'd just then discovered that the word "world" could have come from the Frisian word "Wrâlda." So I told her it was Wrâlda working hard in the basement to bring us water. So she then called our place Wralda and we liked it too. Wish I'd never used Long Look.[2]

The actual writing is now done in a small, one room cabin that Manfred calls the "Teepee" or, in less affectionate moments, "The Shack." In this cabin, about ten by fourteen feet, reside his battered old typewriter, notes, and manuscripts on a desk made out of an old door. Memorabilia, maps, and unassorted odds and ends make their home at various points on the unpainted walls or wooden floor. A shelf over the window contains a row of his books. Closeby are dictionaries and some files. Along the wall over the desk are several shelves stuffed with favorite books.

C) Impression figures and price: Publishers have become notoriously reluctant to disclose sales figures and other documents can be unreliable. By a careful study of these documents (newspaper articles, private letters, press notices) and with the aid of Manfred's careful files and reliable memory, impression figures are provided which are reasonably accurate. In cases where publishers have released figures to the authors, their figure is entered with notation as such.

D) Notes on the writing and publishing history of the work.

3) SUBSEQUENT EDITIONS:

The third major entry under each Original Book provides in lesser detail all subsequent editions of the book, including foreign and paperback editions.

---

[2]From a personal letter to the authors, September 1979.

Original Books

A1 THE GOLDEN BOWL 1944

a. A NOVEL BY FEIKE FEIKEMA / rule / The / Golden / Bowl / rule / THE WEBB PUBLISHING COMPANY / Saint Paul -- 1944

(21 x 13 cm), 121 leaves, pp. [i] - [x], [1] - [2], 3-226, [227] - [230].

Contents: [i] blank; [ii] blank; [iii] THE GOLDEN BOWL; [iv] blank; [v] Title Page; [vi] Copyright page (1944), identification of first edition, and other publisher's matter; [vii] Dedication: This first one is for / John W. Huizenga / who trimmed and fuelled / the flame; [viii] blank; [ix] quotation from Arthur Machen, Hieroglyphics; [x] blank; [1] THE GOLDEN BOWL; [2] blank; 3-226 text; [227] - [230] blank.

Identification of first edition on copyright page [vi].

Cover: Light gray cloth on pressed boards. Front and back blank. Spine: The / Golden / Bowl [gold letters inside a blue rectangle] / Feike / Feikema [blue letters] / rule / WEBB [gold letters inside a blue rectangle].

Dust Jacket: Front and spine are gold. On top half of front: The / Golden / Bowl [in blue letters and script style of title page] / A NOVEL BY [blue letters] / Feike Feikema [white letters in a blue rectangle]. Spine: Title / author / publisher [in same design as cover]. Back: half page photo of Manfred followed by book review blurbs. Front flap: price in upper right, $2.50, followed by blurb on the novel. Back flap: continues review blurbs from back cover, two paragraphs of biographical data on author at bottom.

Place of Composition: Final draft at 1814 4th St. S.E.
                        Minneapolis

Published September, 1944 in an impression of 3,000 copies. Price: $2.50.

Notes: As his first published novel, The Golden Bowl is the one on which, as Manfred says, he "cut his teeth." The publishing story is detailed at some length in the narrative interview at the conclusion of this study.
    The idea for the novel originated from Manfred's hitchhiking

trip across the drought-sticken and depression-ridden western states in 1934 (see entry for The Wind Blows Free). The first draft was written in 1937 while Manfred was working as a reporter for the Minneapolis Journal.

The novel went through seven drafts, listed here under their working titles:
1) "Of These It Is Said," Novel, 150 pages.
2) "Of These It Is Said," Three Act Play, 134 pages.
3) "Of These It Is Said," One Act Play, 64 pages.
4) "Of These It Is Said," Novel, 143 pages.
5) "The Golden Bowl is Broken," Novel, 220 pages.
6) "The Golden Bowl is Broken," Novel, 220 pages.
7) "The Golden Bowl is Broken," Novel, 169 pages.

The "is Broken" from the title was not removed until the galleys where it is penciled out. Also, until the galleys the book had been dedicated to John W. Huizenga and James M. Shields. On the galleys Shield's name is penciled out and subsequently the first edition of This is the Year was dedicated to Shields and to Manfred's father.

b. The Golden Bowl. Saint Paul: The Webb Publishing Company, 1944. Second impression of the first edition.

The second impression of the Webb first edition has enough changes in book form to warrant its own entry. Most evident is the reduction in size to 19.5 x 12.5 cm. The paper is considerably thinner. The cloth cover is changed from a heavy quality buckram to a thinner texture, although cover design is in all respects the same. This impression is run from the same plates and type size and other inside matter is the same as the first impression. The second impression is identified as such on the copyright page [vi].

The second impression may be further identified by the dust jacket. Instead of gold this is a bright yellow. Design remains identical except for the inside flaps which include more recent review blurbs.

The second impression was in a run of 2,500 copies.

c. The Golden Bowl. New York: Grosset and Dunlap, 1944.

The Grosset and Dunlap edition was published by arrangement

Original Books 21

with the Webb Publishing Company and uses the Webb plates. The text is the same. Although the copyright page [vi] gives the date of 1944, the Grosset and Dunlap edition was not run until 1946.

The book bears slight differences from the Webb edition. Size is 19 x 13 cm. The title page reads: A NOVEL BY FEIKE FEIKEMA / rule / The / Golden / Bowl [in script letters identical to Webb edition] / Grosset and Dunlap emblem / GROSSET & DUNLAP / Publishers New York / Published by arrangement with The Webb Publishing Company. The cover is orange cloth on pressed boards. Spine reads: The / Golden / Bowl / Feike / Feikema / Grosset / & Dunlap.

The dust jacket is in tones of red and gold against a black background. Illustration in center of front cover depicts a bleached skull on a prairie, a farm in the distance, a sky in red. At center, in gold letters: The / Golden / Bowl. At bottom, in red letters: FEIKE FEIKEMA. Spine includes author in red letters, title in gold letters, publisher in red letters. Back cover has a photo of Manfred at a typewriter. Front flap: the blurb on the novel differs from the Webb edition and includes the following note at bottom of flap:

> The issuance of this COMPLETE
> AND UNABRIDGED NEW EDITION
> at a reduced price is made possible by
> (a) use of the same plates made for
> the original edition; (b) acceptance
> by the author of a reduced royalty.

Back flap has review blurbs and publisher's address.

The Grosset & Dunlap impression was in a run of 10,000 copies. Price: $1.00.

d. The Golden Bowl. London: Dennis Dobson Limited, 1947. 240 pages. Price: 8s 6d net.

Cover: Green cloth on pressed boards. Front and back blank. Spine: title, author, publisher in gold letters.

Dust jacket: Jacket design includes spine in gold. Front has in

brown tones the faces of a man and woman. At top: THE /
GOLDEN / BOWL [white letters]. At bottom: Feike Feikema
[white letters]. Spine has title, author, publisher.

e. The Golden Bowl. Vermillion, South Dakota: The University of
South Dakota Press, 1969.
Price: $4.00.
Cover: Yellow cloth on pressed boards. Front and back blank.
Spine has title in black rectangle, author, publisher.

Dust jacket: Front: white with circle of gold in center. Inside
the circle: The / Golden / Bowl. Below circle: Frederick Manfred.
At top of jacket: A Novel of South Dakota. At bottom of jacket:
Introduction by John R. Milton / Twenty-fifth Anniversary
Edition. Spine duplicates cover but with title in a gold rectangle.
Back is blank white.

This special 25th anniversary edition of The Golden Bowl was in
an impression of 3,000 copies, of which 1,000 were bound in cloth
and 2,000 bound in paper.

Note: The opening two and a half pages of this edition were
put entirely in the present tense to match or balance the last
pages of the book. The effort here was to put the past inside
the book in a present tense frame.

f. The Golden Bowl. Albuquerque: The University of New Mexico
Press, a Zia Book, 1976 [Paperback]. 226 pages.
Original price: $3.45 entered on upper left of back cover; later
changed to $3.95 by placing a price sticker over original price.

Cover: In half tones of brown and gray, cover depicts a windmill
in a drought-stricken landscape. Artist's signature is at lower
portion of windmill as: Stouffer, 76. Front cover has at upper
left: A Zia Book; at left center: The / Golden / Bowl / Frederick
Manfred [all letters in black]. Spine has Zia emblem, author, title,
publisher. Back cover gives price in upper left and blurb.

Note: This is a reprinting of the University of South Dakota edition
with a slightly revised introduction by John R. Milton. This edition
retains the textual revision changing the first 2½ pages to present
tense.

A2 BOY ALMIGHTY 1945

a. Boy Almighty / rule / A NOVEL BY / rule / FEIKE FEIKEMA / Itasca Press Emblem / The Itasca Press / A DIVISION OF THE WEBB PUBLISHING COMPANY / Saint Paul: 1945

(19.6 x 13 cm) 176 leaves, pp. [i] - [x], xi-xii, [1] - 338, [339] - [340].

Contents: [i] blank; [ii] blank; [iii] BOY ALMIGHTY; [iv] ALSO BY FEIKE FEIKEMA / THE GOLDEN BOWL; [v] Title Page; [vi] Copyright (1945), identification of first edition and other publisher's matter; [vii] Dedication: For Maryanna Shorba / friend and wife; [viii] blank; [ix] quotation from Whitman; [x] blank; xi-xii Contents; [1] -338 Text; [339] - [340] blank.

Identification of first edition on copyright page [vi].

Cover: Light green cloth on pressed boards. Front and back blank. Spine: BOY ALMIGHTY [inside red rectangular device] / Feike Feikema [blue letters] / THE / ITASCA / PRESS / WEBB [blue letters].

Dust Jacket: Against a green background, the jacket design includes the following inside a large red circle: Boy Almighty [white letters] / A NOVEL BY [black letters] / FEIKE FEIKEMA [white letters] / WINNER OF / AMERICAN ACADEMY AWARD / 1945 [black letters]. Spine duplicates lettering of cover. Back has a photo of Manfred at typewriter which was also used on the Webb edition of The Golden Bowl. Blurb on author follows photo. Front flap gives price in upper right, $2.75, and blurb follows. Back flap continues blurb.

Place of Composition: First draft at 1814 4th St. S.E.
　　　　　　　　　　　　　　　　Minneapolis

　　　　　　　　　Final draft at Wrâlda
　　　　　　　　　　　　Bloomington, Minnesota

Published November, 1945 in one impression of 2,500 copies.

Price: $2.75.

b. Boy Almighty. London: Dennis Dobson, Ltd., 1950.
Price: 10s 6d net.

Cover: Black cloth on pressed boards. Front and back blank. Spine has title, author, publisher in gold letters.

Dust jacket: Cover design includes spine. Against a red background, cover illustration depicts a young man looking out of a window and touching leaves. Illustration is in tones of yellow and white. At top: FEIKE FEIKEMA / AUTHOR OF THE CHOKECHERRY TREE. At bottom: BOY ALMIGHTY. Spine has title, author, and publisher in white. Back of jacket has advertising for other books.

c. Ragazzo Onnipotente. Trans. Maria Celletti Marzano. Milano: Tip Siata, Garzanti, 1950 [Paperback]. 410 pages.
Price: 600 lire.

Cover has a photo of a man superimposed against a photo of mountains. At center of cover in an orange rectangle: FEIKE FEIKEMA / RAGAZZO / ONNIPOTENTE. At lower right: "AMENA" / GARZANTI / LIRE 600. Back cover has a list of books in Garzanti series.

A3 THIS IS THE YEAR 1947

a. FEIKE FEIKEMA / This is the Year / DOUBLEDAY & COMPANY, INC. / GARDEN CITY, NEW YORK -- 1947.

(21 x 14.5 cm), 314 leaves, pp. [i] - [vi], vii-viii, [ix] - [x], xi-xiv, [1] - [3], 4-623, [624] - [626].

Contents: [i] THIS IS THE YEAR; [ii] blank; [iii] Title page; [iv] Copyright (1947), identification of first edition, and other publisher's matter; [v] Dedication: For my father, / FEIKE (FRANK) FEIKEMA; / for my friend, / JAMES M. SHIELDS: [vi] blank; vii-viii Contents; [ix] Acknowledgment [financial assistance from Regional Fellowships of University of Minnesota]; [x] blank; xi-xiv PRELUDE; [1] BOOK ONE; [2] -614 Text; [615]-616 POSTLUDE; [617]-623 GLOSSARY / of unusual words and phrases (most of them Frisian) / which appear in the text of the novel; [624]-[626] blank.

Identification of first edition on Copyright page [iv].

Original Books

Cover: Inside endleaves and cover, front and back, is a map of Pier's farm and neighborhood in Siouxland. Cover is brown cloth on pressed boards. Front and back blank. Spine: FEIKE FEIKEMA [gold letters] / blue and gold rules / This / is / the / Year [gold letters in a blue rectangle] / blue and gold rules / Doubleday [gold letters].

Dust jacket: Cover design includes spine. A five centimeter border in green runs along top and bottom. Center is brown with thin yellow stripes along edge. Front: At top in green border a quotation: "He is in his early thirties. It is apparent that he may / become one of the most important novelists in America" / SINCLAIR LEWIS. At Center: FEIKE FEIKEMA [white letters] / This is / the Year [yellow letters] / A NOVEL OF FAITH IN THE EARTH. At bottom in green border a quotation: "I don't know when I have met a mind that I feel more / sure of, that strikes me as so big and full in every way." / VAN WYCK BROOKS. Spine: FEIKE FEIKEMA / This is / the Year / Doubleday. Back: Photo of Manfred by Bruce Sifford. Blurb follows. Front flap: in upper right, Price, $3.00. Blurb follows. Rear flap: under heading ABOUT THIS BOOK notes are supplied that detail the chronology of weather patterns Manfred kept while working on the book.

Place of composition: First draft written at 1814 4th St., S.E.
                                        Minneapolis, Minnesota
              Final draft written at Wrâlda
                                        Bloomington, Minnesota

Published March, 1947 in an impression of 8,500 copies. A second impression of 6,000 copies followed [figures confirmed by Doubleday].

Price: $3.00.

Notes: This is the Year was written intermittently at the same time as The Golden Bowl. After the first rejection of the unfinished draft (about 70 pages) of The Golden Bowl in 1937, Manfred set it aside to begin work on This is the Year. The two books were crafted side by side. Tired of one or discouraged by rejections, Manfred would work on the other in various rooming houses in Dinkytown near the University of Minnesota. This is the Year thereby went through three drafts. At one point in the writing, frustrated by the progress of the work, Manfred burned a sizeable portion of the novel. It was, in Manfred's estimation, "carpentry work rather than the real kind of finished woodwork that a real woodworker does" (<u>Conversations</u>, p. 87).

Clearly, the novel lacked a compelling unity to knit the narrative plot (as more than one publisher pointed out to the author-- see the narrative interview at the conclusion of this bibliography). The novel was strongly and naturally related to weather patterns as they affected the life of the farmer. With greater deliberation Manfred tried to capture the natural rhythms of weather patterns in the flow and pace of the narrative. For this, he studied meteorological patterns in Iowa for the years 1918 to 1936, focusing finally on a five year period. That became, as Manfred said, "my ground plan." In terms of the saying "warp and woof" in which "warp" refers to the pattern of the fabric and "woof" refers to the fabric itself, Manfred considered the weather as the "warp" of the book and the characters as the "woof."

b. dit is it jier. Trans. Klaes Dykstra [into Frisian]. Drachten: Drukkerij en utjowerij Laverman, N.V., 1967. 658 pages.
Price: fl 22.90
Cover: Dark blue cloth on pressed boards. Lettering on front reads: dit is / it jier [gold letters]. Spine has title and author in gold.

Dust jacket: Color is deep blue. A line of birds in flight form a top border. In center, a circle of green and white with two birds on a branch. Bottom left: dit / is it jier [white letters] / FREDERICK MANFRED [red letters]. Spine: title and author vertically. Back: upper border of birds in flight continues. The rest of the back jacket is blank white. Front flap: photo of Manfred and blurb. Rear flap: continues blurb with notes on author.

c. This is the Year. Boston: Gregg Press, 1979.

Price: $14.95

This edition, issued in September, 1979, is part of The Gregg Press Western Fiction Series. Gregg Press is a division of G.K. Hall & Co.

The impression is a photographic reprint of the Doubleday text.

This edition differs in size from the Doubleday edition and measures 21.6 x 13 cm. All front matter differs from the original to reflect the new edition. The copyright page [iv] gives publishing information on this text, notice of arrangements with Doubleday and the author, identification of first printing (September, 1979), and other publisher's matter. The edition includes an Introduction by Max Westbrook (pp. v-vii), and includes an updated map of the Siouxland region (p. [viii]). In the Dedication James M. Shield's name is removed and this edition is dedicated only to Manfred's father, using the father's true name Feike Feikes Feikema VI.

The cover is cloth on pressed boards. Front and back are blank. Spine reads: MANFRED / This is the Year [vertically] / Gregg emblem / GREGG [all lettering in gold].

The dust jacket is tan paper with impressed chain-lines. Front of jacket has the Siouxland map of p. [viii] in a circle at center. At top: This is the Year [brown letters]. At bottom: Frederick Manfred [brown letters] / With a new introduction by Max Westbrook [black letters]. Spine of dust jacket duplicates book cover. Back of dust jacket lists 15 titles in the Gregg Western Fiction Series including this one. Front flap has a blurb on novel. Rear flap has blurbs on Manfred and Max Westbrook. First printed November, 1979 in an impression of 750 copies.

A4 THE CHOKECHERRY TREE 1948

a. THE CHOKECHERRY TREE / by Feike Feikema / DOUBLEDAY & COMPANY, INC. / Garden City, New York, 1948

(20.2 x 13.6 cm), 144 leaves [untrimmed], [I]-[II], [i]-[x], xi-xii, [xiii]-[xiv], [1]-270, [271]-[272].

Contents: [I] blank; [II] blank; [i] THE CHOKECHERRY TREE; [ii] list of last four books by author including this one; [iii] title page; [iv] Copyright (1948) and other publisher's matter; [v] Dedication: for PAUL C. HILLESTAD / ELOF DIDN'T GET THE BREAK I DID -- YOU WEREN'T / THERE TO REACH OUT A HAND TO HELP HIM UP; [vi] blank; [vii] Author's disclaimer; [viii] blank; [ix] quotations from Chaucer and E.J. Simmons;

[x] blank; xi-xii contents; [xiii] THE CHOKECHERRY TREE; [xiv] blank; [1]-270 text; [271]-[272] blank.

Identification of first edition on copyright page [iv].

Cover: Gray cloth on pressed boards. Front and back blank. Spine: FEIKE FEIKEMA [red letters] / rule / The / Choke- / cherry / Tree [gray letters in a red rectangle] / rule / Doubleday [red letters].

Dust Jacket: Jacket design includes spine. In tones of blue and yellow jacket design depicts Elof holding a suitcase and coat while walking down a highway. A truck is in the distance. The roadsign identifies the town as HELLO. Other details include a water tower, gas station, gas pumps, grain stacks, etc. In the foreground are pen and ink images of a girl, a man smoking a pipe, and a tree without leaves. At top: FEIKE FEIKEMA / author of THIS IS THE YEAR [yellow letters]. THE / CHOKECHERRY / TREE [white letters]. Spine: FEIKE / FEIKEMA / THE CHOKE- / CHERRY / TREE / Doubleday. Back of jacket has a photo of Manfred at typewriter on upper half. Bottom half has brief biographical note and quotations from Sinclair Lewis and Van Wyck Brooks. Front flap: at upper right the price, $2.75. Blurb follows. Back flap: a puff for This is the Year with quotations from reviews.

Place of composition: Wrâlda at Bloomington, Minnesota
Summer, 1946 and early 1947

Published April, 1948 in an impression of 6,500 copies. [Impression figures confirmed by Doubleday].
Price: $2.75.
Notes: The Chokecherry Tree started as a short story which flowed into a pattern of four more short stories. With the five stories finished, Manfred rewrote them to form a base for this novel. The character of Elof Lofblom is a composite, drawn partly from a friend, partly from Manfred's own life, particularly the summer of 1936, the drought year, when he was out of work, and "when he felt small with big feet" (Manfred's note). The story of the discovery of Elof's name is recounted in Conversations with Manfred (p. 57). Similarly, Gert is a composite of several girls which taken together represented for Manfred "an earth mother"

Original Books 29

to Elof.
The Chokecherry Tree was accepted immediately for publication.

b. The Chokecherry Tree. London: Dennis Dobson, 1949.
Price: 9s 6d net.

Cover: light gray cloth on pressed boards. Front and back blank. Spine has title, author, and publisher in red letters.

Dust Jacket: Tones of light green and brown. Variations in white. The chokecherry tree runs along spine and over upper left of cover. The design depicts Elof on right hand side of page carrying a suitcase down a road. In the distance a man and woman hold hands. In upper left at an angle: THE / CHOKECHERRY / TREE [white letters]. Bottom left: FEIKE FEIKEMA. Flaps have blurb.

c. El Cerezo. Trans. Jesus Pardo. Madrid: Colercion "La Nave," 1949.

This edition of The Chokecherry Tree was pirated and later was settled with Manfred's agent, Curtis Brown, Ltd.

d. The Chokecherry Tree. Denver: Alan Swallow, 1961.
Price: $3.75

Cover: light red cloth on pressed boards. Front and back blank.
Spine: THE CHOKECHERRY TREE / MANFRED [vertically] / Swallow.

Dust Jacket: Jacket design includes spine. A red field on lower two-thirds of jacket is broken in two by an irregular vertical band of white. Top third is white. A line drawing of a chokecherry tree with scattered white and black berries runs vertically across cover. Upper right has in rough drawn letters: THE [black letters] / CHOKE [black letters] / Cherry [red letters] / TREE [black letters]. Running vertically on left: FREDERICK MANFRED. Spine has title, author, and publisher. Back is blank white. Flaps have blurb.

From an impression run of 750 copies, 500 were bound in cloth.

Note: A letter forming one of the italic introductions to each chapter was removed. The letter was addressed to the presidents and "potentates" of the world. The edition was repaginated.

e. The Chokecherry Tree. Denver: Alan Swallow, 1961 [paperback]. Price: $1.85.

Note: This is a paperback edition in the Swallow paperbooks series. In design and format it is identical to the hardcover edition. From the 750 copy impression run, 250 copies were bound in paperback.

f. The Chokecherry Tree. Albuquerque: University of New Mexico Press, A Zia Book, 1975 [paperback]. 260 pages. Price: $2.95.

Cover: Light green paper. Bottom half of front depicts in half tones a pen and ink drawing of a chokecherry tree, a farm and a crossroads. Top left: A Zia Book. Center: The / Chokecherry / Tree / Frederick / Manfred. Spine has author, title, publisher. Back has price and blurbs.

Notes: This paperback edition is shot from the Doubleday plates. Pagination differs (266 total pages) and size (20.2 x 13.5 cm.). This edition contains an Introduction (pp. vii-xii) by Delbert E. Wylder that supplies biographical information on Manfred and some critical observations on the book.

A5 THE PRIMITIVE 1949

a. THE PRIMITIVE / Feike Feikema / Doubleday Anchor Emblem / GARDEN CITY, N.Y. / Doubleday & Company, Inc. / 1949.

(21.2 x 14 cm), 240 leaves [untrimmed], pp. [I]-[II], [i]-[vi], vii-[viii], ix-x, [xi]-[xvi], [1]-460, [461]-[462].

Contents: [I] blank; [II] blank; [i] The Primitive; [ii] list of last five books by author including this one; [iii] title page; [iv] Copyright (1949) and other publisher's matter; [v] Dedication: This first volume is for / HELEN OF TROY / and PROFESSOR W.H.J. [Note: "Helen of Troy" refers to Helen Reitsema Vander Meer, "Professor W.H.J." refers to Professor William Harry Jellema]; [vi] blank; vii Note on format for World's Wanderer Trilogy; [viii] blank; ix-x quotations from Homer, Charles M. Doughty, Job [in Frisian Bible], Talmud; [xi] Acknowledgment letters] / A novel by / FREDERICK / F. / MANFRED. Spine: Frederick F. / Manfred / LORD GRIZZLY [vertically in brown letters] / McGraw-Hill. Back: Photo of Manfred, notes on author, and review blurbs. Publisher's address at bottom. Front flap: Price in upper right, $3.75. Blurb follows. At bottom attribution of jacket design to Arthur Shilstone. Back flap continues blurb. One paragraph blurb on author. Note on bottom of back flap reads: Illustrated with endpaper maps.

Place of composition: At Wrâlda

Published September, 1954 in an impression of 5,000 copies. A second unidentified impression of 3,000 copies and a third unidentified impression of 3,000 copies followed.

Price: $3.75.

Notes: The writing of Lord Grizzly constitutes one of the most startling, and well-recorded, efforts of Manfred's career. The story is amply detailed in a number of interviews including a lengthy section of Conversations (pp. 105-131) and a very illuminating discussion in "West of the Mississippi: An Interview with Frederick Manfred," Critique, II (Winter, 1959), pp. 35-36. Additional new material is supplied in the narrative interview at the conclusion of this study.

Clearly, the period during which Lord Grizzly was written was one of artistic frustration for Manfred, a frustration accentuated by the mixed critical reception given the World's Wanderer Trilogy. There were many positive reviews of the work (Christopher Matthews in The Milwaukee Journal: "adventures that have hardly been surpassed since Chaucer"). The negative reviews, however, were particularly vitriolic. Max Gissen, Hal Borland, Granville Hicks, Paul Corey, all major figures in the New York reviewing world of the 1950's, ranged from simply negative to savage in their assessments.

Critics have also speculated on the role of Manfred's name change in 1952 from Frederick Feikema to Frederick Feikema Manfred. Before 1952 Feike Feikema was used as a penname. His family name in Frisian would have been Feike Feikes Feikema. It may be interesting to speculate that for someone as concerned about place and people as Manfred, the name-change cannot be taken lightly. It may be considered akin to a spiritual conversion, and Lord Grizzly its testament. It is true that Manfred believed the former heroes of his fiction were too "thin," and he deliberately sought a hero who was at once complex in himself but who also would stir archetypal associations with the classical tradition of heroes.

But the name-change and its effect on Manfred's writing must be qualified. By Manfred's account, he had wanted to make the change since 1944 when he started using the penname of Feike Feikema. It wasn't until the winter of 1949-50 that Professor Konstantin Reichardt, a linguist at the University of Minnesota and at Yale, found out for him that Feikema translated could be construed as Fredman, or Frederickman, or Manfred. Manfred suggested the change to his wife Maryanna, spent the better part of a year reflecting on it, and went ahead with the change in 1952.

Many accounts of Lord Grizzly assert that the work was researched in one year and written the next. This is an oversimplification and only partly true. Manfred first ran across the story of Hugh Glass in the South Dakota in the summer of 1943. One of the problems he had in writing the novel, Manfred has said, is that he did not know how to write convincingly about a man who forgives. Not until the early 50's did he run into a case where a relative (not his brother as Robert Wright reports in his book Frederick Manfred) "forgave" the law because he felt that "the law had made an honest mistake." The act moved him profoundly, gave him an insight on how to conclude the Hugh Glass story, and in Manfred's words "really put the socks into my research reading."

Lord Grizzly is Manfred's best selling novel. In former years publishers proclaimed impression figures with all the fervor of evangelists. Our age has seen a switch. Wrenching impression figures from a publisher now is akin to prying a tooth from the mouth of a shark. Manfred himself has lost count of the numbers of copies of Lord Grizzly. "Millions," he has said recently. He may be right. Russell Roth reported in The Minneapolis Sunday Tribune (August 1, 1954) that the Pocket Book paperback edition was in a run of 250,000 copies (for which Manfred received a flat fee of $5,000). Signet took over the rights in 1964, and has run 13 impressions.

Lord Grizzly will be published again in hardcover by Gregg Press in 1980 as a part of the reprinting of the entire Buckskin Man Series in the Gregg Press Western Fiction Series.

Original Books 37

b. Lord Grizzly. New York: Pocket Books, Inc., Cardinal, 1955 [Paperback, C-192]. 304 pages.

Price: 35¢.

This Cardinal edition is shot from new plates and reset type. The first printing was in October, 1955. By January, 1957 a third printing had been run.

The cover design is from a painting by Clark Hulings and depicts Hugh Glass (painted to look like Manfred) crawling across a rocky bluff. He is dressed in bucksins and a fur hat. Across the center of cover scenes from the novel are depicted. At top, in a gold vertical rectangle on left: C-192 / The Cardinal emblem, 35¢ / A / CARDINAL / EDITION. At top against a tan background: "The like of this we have seldom seen since THE BIG SKY." / -- THE NEW YORK TIMES / LORD / GRIZZLY / The story of a frontierman's epic courage to survive and / his terrible vengeance against those who left him to die. At center right: FREDERICK F. / MANFRED. At bottom left: THE COMPLETE BOOK.

c. Lord Grizzly. London: Transworld Publishers, Corgi Books, 1957 [Paperback].

Price: 3s 6d net

Cover design depicts a mountain man kneeling behind a rock bluff and holding a knife. From below Indians are in pursuit. Background is in yellow. At top left, inside Corgi emblem: CORGI / GIANT / 3'6. At upper right: FREDERICK MANFRED / LORD / GRIZZLY [blue letters] / A story of a frontierman's / epic struggle for survival and his / terrible vengeance against / those who left him to die . . . . Spine has numbers G438 at top, title, author, publisher. Back cover depicts mountain man wrestling a grizzly bear.

d. Lord Grizzly. New York: New American Library, Signet, 1964 [paperback]. 270 pages.
First printing, March, 1964.

This paperback edition was issued under two different cover designs to reflect an increase in price.

d1) Signet P2437, Price: 60¢.
Against a white background the cover depicts in the foreground a mountain man holding a rifle. Behind him scenes from the book are depicted, including a grizzly, an Indian woman, and Hugh Glass crawling. At top is the identification: Signet P2437 60¢ Signet emblem. At center in blue letters: LORD / GRIZZLY / FREDERICK MANFRED / The mountain men were a breed apart among / the trappers and scouts of the American fron- / tier. This magnificent novel tells of / their extra-ordinary adventures / and boundless courage.

d2) Signet 451 W6979, Price: $1.50.

Cover illustration depicts a mountain man facing a large grizzly in foreground. The mountain man is holding a bowie knife and a long pointed stick. Background is shaded gray and tan sky. At top is the identification Signet 451 W6979 $1.50 Signet emblem. In white letters bordered by black: FREDERICK MANFRED / LORD / GRIZZLY / The magnificent saga of Hugh Glass, a man whose / extraordinary adventure and boundless courage became / one of the mightiest legends of the American frontier. Cover illustration is signed Len McCance.

e. Lord Grizzly. Trans. Maria Luisa Cesa Bianchi. Milano: Longanesi & C., 1977 [paperback]. 202 pages.

Price: 1000 lire.

Cover design is on brown glossy paper. Cover illustration, inside a 9.5 x 8.5 centimeter rectangle on bottom half of cover, depicts a grizzly bear standing over a prone man. Dogs are attacking the grizzly. At top left: the Longanesi western classics series emblem. At top center: I CLASSICI DEL WEST / SUPER [yellow letters] / Un romanzo di [white letters] / FREDERICK MANFRED [yellow letters] / LORD GRIZZLY [yellow letters]. At bottom: Longanesi & C. Back cover has blurb on Manfred and price.

f. Lord Grizzly: The Legend of Hugh Glass.
An unpublished screenplay by Manfred written in 1965. The manuscript consists of 126 leaves and is reposited in the University of South Dakota Libraries, and also in the manuscripts collection at the University of Minnesota Library.

A9 MORNING RED 1956

a. MORNING RED / a romance / FREDERICK MANFRED / ALAN SWALLOW, Denver / 1956

(21.7 x 14 cm.), 310 leaves, pp. [1] - [9] 10 - 617 [618] - [620]

Contents: [1] MORNING RED / a romance; [2] list of last nine works by author including this one; [3] title page: [4] Copyright (1956) and other publisher's matter; [5] Dedication: For WILLIAM FAULKNER / neighbor living down the valley a piece / and also a son of the Father of Waters; [6] blank; [7] - [8] Contents: [9] Part One [epigraph from a folk saying]; 10-616 Text; 617 ABOUT THE AUTHOR [618] - [620] blank.

No identification of first edition.

Cover: Red cloth on pressed boards. Front: reproduces title page in black letters but omits publisher. Spine: title, author, publisher in reduced type of title page. Back blank.

Dust Jacket: "morning red" in red script letters centered. A MAJOR AMERICAN NOVEL in lower center. Frederick Manfred in lower right. Cover illustration, from a drawing by Manfred, includes spine. The lower third depicts a gray field with wired telephone poles angling from lower left to upper right horizon of gray field. Upper two thirds deepen from light pink at center to red at top. Spine: MORNING RED / Manfred / Swallow. Back Cover has small photo of Manfred and three paragraph quotation from William Carlos Williams under heading: WHAT ONE CRITIC SAID ABOUT MANFRED'S PREVIOUS BOOK, LORD GRIZZLY. Inside front and back flap a blurb on the novel with publisher's address on bottom back flap.

Note: One hundred copies of the dust jacket are marked MINNESOTA CENTENNIAL EDITION in white letters across top. The copies are in all other respects the same.

Place and date of composition: At Wrâlda, Minneapolis
20 April, 1951 to December 1952;
March, 1954 to June, 1955, and
February, 1956.

Published September, 1956 in an impression of 1,500 copies.

Price: $6.00.

b. MORNING RED, Denver: Alan Swallow, 1956 [paperback].

This paperback edition was shot from the original plates and the text is the same. The page size is slightly smaller (21 x 13.5 cm.) but the type size is the same.

Cover: Front: design depicts buildings in outline across bottom and a series of horizontal lines of black clouds covering approximately the bottom two-thirds of cover. In upper right: MORNING [in black letters] / RED [in red letters] / by FREDRICK [sic] MANFRED. Beneath author: Swallow emblem and A SWALLOW PAPERBOOK / 1.95. Spine: title, author [spelled correctly], and publisher. Back has blurb on Manfred and a list of Swallow Paperbooks. Cover design attributed to Lowell Naeve. One impression of 500 copies.
Price $1.95

Notes: Manfred often refers to Morning Red as the novel in which he "went the deepest." It is a complex work, arranging multiple and interweaving plots. Part of this can be explained by the fact that the novel evolved from two unpublished manuscripts "The Rape of Elizabeth" and "The Mountain of Myrrh." In Conversations with Manfred the author relates that while talking about the manuscripts with Russell Roth, Roth commented that the two had a similar tone. Manfred thought at first of rewriting the two manuscripts to conflate them into one work. Manfred commented in his interview with James Lee (Studies in the Novel, 5, Fall, 1973, pp. 358-382) that the new work went badly and that finally he "burned some of it, I locked the rest away, and I started from scratch." Echoes of the earlier manuscripts nonetheless remain. Jack Nagel, for example, does rape Elizabeth. With the fresh start, however, the new work developed rapidly. In a private, unpublished letter (December 1, 1954) Manfred reported to a friend that he was on a new book which was 850 pages in draft --"though the end is in sight." Considering all the various manuscripts that went into the making of Morning Red, Manfred commented in a newspaper interview that "I wrote a total of some 4,000 to get the 600 which now make up Morning Red. I cut out all kinds of implausible characters who were true in real life because I wanted, if possible, a work of art besides merely the truth." (Manfred Tells About Characters in

Original Books 41

His New Novel, 'Morning Red,' " The Minneapolis Sunday Tribune, December 16, 1956).

With the huge success of Lord Grizzly the cool reception publishers gave to Morning Red is surprising. Eastern publishers systematically rejected the work (about 20 rejections in all). Manfred wrote to Alan Swallow and eventually showed him the work. Swallow's reaction is recounted in his "The Mavericks," Critique: Studies in Modern Fiction, 2 (Winter, 1959), 74-92.

The original manuscripts of The Rape of Elizabeth and The Mountain of Myrrh are in the Manfred Collection at the University of Minnesota.

A10 RIDERS OF JUDGMENT, 1957

a. Riders / of Judgment / Frederick Manfred / Random House / Random House Emblem / New York.

(20.3 x 13.6 cm.) 190 leaves. pp. [i] - [viii], [1] - [2], [3] - 368, [369] - [372].

Contents: [i] Riders of Judgment; [ii] List of last ten works by Manfred including this one; [iii] Title page; [iv] Copyright (1957), identification of first printing, and other publisher's matter; [v] Dedication: For William Carlos Williams / who is hacking out a new road up ahead, / all the while singing his tender is the North. / Anonymous [Tennyson]; [viii] blank; [1] Riders of tender is the North. / Anonymous; [viii] blank; [1] Riders of Judgment; [2] blank; [3] - 368 text; [369] blank; [370] ABOUT THE AUTHOR [371] - [372] blank.

Identification of first edition as "First Printing" on copyright page [iv].

Cover: Light brown cloth on pressed boards. Front has Random House Emblem in right center. Back blank. Spine: A large gold star / Frederick Manfred [green letters] / Riders / of / Judgment [gold letters inside a green rectangle] / Random House [green letters] / large gold star.

Dust Jacket: Cover design includes spine. Against a white background the front cover depicts a steer head at top, a noose from top to center, a rifle and saddle at center, sketch of mountains across lower center. At top: A classic novel of the West [green letters]. At center: Riders of / JUDGMENT. At Bottom: by FREDERICK MANFRED / author of LORD GRIZZLY [green letters]. Spine has a spur and revolver at top. At center: RIDERS / of JUDGMENT [green letters] / Frederick / Manfred / Random House Emblem / RANDOM / HOUSE [green letters]. Back cover has photo of Manfred by Don Berg and biographical blurb same as page [370] of text. Front flap: At upper right: Price $3.95. Blurb on novel follows. Jacket design attributed to Mitch Havemeyer and Hoyt Howard. Publisher's address at bottom. Back flap continues biographical information from back of jacket.

Place and date of composition: Wrâlda
December 8, 1956

First Edition in an impression of 6,500 copies [impression number confirmed by Random House].

Price: $3.95.

Notes: By the time he wrote Lord Grizzly Manfred had already determined to do a series of novels on the 19th century west. A piece of that west had to be the Cattleman Times, and he chose to write on the period of conflict created by the threat of the nesters and the railroad to the empires of the cattle barons. The story of Riders of Judgment began to form for Manfred after reading an account of Nate Champion in Mercer's The Banditti of the Plains. His research began with investigation into Nate Champion around Kaycee, Wyoming (near Buffalo, Wyoming). Nate Champion became Cain Hammett of the novel.

The novel developed rapidly in the writing. Manfred's customary practice is to write during the morning hours, from about seven a.m. until noon, completing perhaps two to four pages. Riders of Judgment quickly spurted to eight or nine pages a day and the entire last fourth of the novel was written in the space of about two weeks.

b. Riders of Judgment. New York: Pocket Books, Inc., Cardinal, 1958 [paperback C-301]. 344 pages.

Price: 35¢.

Original Books 43

This paperback edition was printed from new plates. The cover illustration is from a painting by A. Leslie Ross. Front cover has against a brown background the faces of three men at right. In center there is an outline of a woman's face. Upper left: A rich, serious novel / of the violent West. At center: RIDERS OF / JUDGMENT [yellow letters]. At lower left: FREDERICK / MANFRED / Author of LORD GRIZZLY. A gold margin at left contains Cardinal Emblem, price, and identifying numbers C-301. Back cover has blurb, a puff for Lloyd C. Douglas' The Robe, and other matter.

c. Jahaci posljednjeg suda. Trans. Milan Crnkovic. Rijeka: O. Kersovani, 1966. 309 pages.

This Yugoslavian edition of Riders of Judgment was arranged by Manfred's agent, Curtis Brown, Ltd., but the author never received royalties on the edition.

d. Riders of Judgment. New York: New American Library, Signet, 1973 [paperback, 451-45505]. 318 pages.

Price: $1.25.

Cover design depicts four men dressed in black riding black horses across a prairie in tones of brown, white and blue. Hills and clouds in the background rise to a blue sky. At upper right: Signet 451-Y5505, $1.25, Signet Emblem. Upper center: FREDERICK MANFRED / RIDERS of / JUDGMENT [white letters] / A rich and roaring novel of the violent West, / by the author of / CONQUERING HORSE and LORD GRIZZLY. Back cover has blurb on novel and note on Manfred.

e. I cavalieri del giudizio. Trans. Giorgio Luxoro. Milano: Longanesi & C., 1976 [paperback]. 290 pages.

Price: 1500 lire.

Cover: Against green glossy paper cover illustration depicts gunman holding revolver on horseback. Upper left: I GRANDI WESTERN / I Cavalieri / del giudizio / di FREDERICK F. MANFRED. Bottom has publisher and price. Back cover has blurb on novel and photo at bottom of John Wayne from a movie clip.

A11 CONQUERING HORSE 1959

a. CONQUERING HORSE / A Novel [in script letters] / McDOWELL, OBOLENSKY / · / NEW YORK.

(20.7 x 14 cm), 223 leaves, pp. [i] - [xii], [1]-[2], 3-353, [354], 355-[356].

Contents: [i] CONQUERING HORSE; [ii] blank; [iii] list of last eleven books by Manfred including this one; [iv] Frederick Manfred [in script letters] / McDowell, Obolensky emblem; [v] title page; [vi] Copyright (1959), identification of First Printing, and other publisher's matter; [vii] Dedication: To Russell Frederick Roth / with borrowed regret; Acknowledgment [to McKnight Foundation for financial support]; [viii] blank; [ix] quotation from D.H. Lawrence, Studies in Classic American Literature; [x] blank; [xi] Contents; [xii] blank; [1] CONQUERING HORSE; [2] blank; 3-353 text; [354] blank; 355 Glossary [of Indian names in book]; [356] ABOUT THE AUTHOR.

Identification of First Printing on Copyright page [vi].

Cover Blue and red cloth on pressed boards [see notes for alternative cover]. Front and back blank. Spine reads: Conquering Horse [vertically in gold letters] / FREDERICK MANFRED [vertically in gold letters] / OBOLENSKY [gold letters].

Dust Jacket: Jacket design includes spine and consists of a blue background with a bottom border of five centimeters in deep red. From top on front of jacket: CONQUERING / HORSE [white letters] / A NOVEL BY / the author of LORD GRIZZLY / and RIDERS OF JUDGMENT / Frederick Manfred [black letters]. At bottom in border: A bold young Sioux wins manhood / and the right to lead his tribe [white letters]. Spine has title [white letters] / author [black letters] / publisher at bottom as: McDOWELL [white letters] / emblem / OBOLENSKY [white letters]. Back has full page photo of Manfred. Front flap gives price in upper right, $4.95, and blurb on novel. Back flap has blurb on Manfred with note that "He is now working away at novel number eleven [sic]."

Place of Composition: At Wrâlda
December 2, 1958

Original Books

Published June, 1959 in an impression of 7,500 copies.
Price: $4.95.

Notes: Critical consensus rates Conquering Horse, along with Lord Grizzly, as one of Manfred's major artistic achievements. In a sense the novel presented greater difficulties than Lord Grizzly. Manfred was particularly conscious of attempting to remain faithful to the Indian spirit, while recognizing well the pretense of an Anglo writer in the attempt. Yet the novel is narrated wholly from within the Indian world, and is generally considered as one of the most faithful testaments to the Indian world-and-life spirit in contemporary literature by a non-Indian author. To see the novel only as an effort to capture the Indian spirit, however, is an error. Manfred's belief is that modern man has lost a sense of the spiritual and his effort in this novel, as in many of his works, is to rekindle this sense universally.

In light of its demonstrated fidelity to Indian spirit, it is curious that this novel involved possibly the least amount of first hand historical research among the Buckskin Man Tales. Compared to Lord Grizzly for which Manfred actually crawled over the rugged western landscape with his leg on a travois, or the later Milk of Wolves for which he lived for a time with a northwoods hermit, Manfred made little such effort at first hand research in Conquering Horse. The research that he did engage is recorded in this excerpt from a letter to the authors of this study dated February 16, 1980:

> It is true that I didn't do too much physical research, certainly not as much as I did for Lord Grizzly. But I did do two very important things. One, I drove down to Red Cloud, Nebraska, to check out the terrain south of town, on the south side of the Republican River. I'd figured out from a contour map I had that there had to be three bluffs close together there. Also, from my readings I had figured out that that was about the last place north (north from Mexico) where a wild stallion might rove. Maryanna went with me. I found the three hills. Took a nap on the middle one. Then, in the evening, we went to visit Mildred Bennett who we had heard had written a book on Willa Cather. Red Cloud was Willa's town. It turns out that Mildred's husband, Wilbur, a doctor, knew where the last stallion had run. His

grandfather was a mustanger. It was dark, moonlight, when he drove me south of town and he stopped at the very bluff where I'd taken a nap! The next day, Maryanna told Mildred and an old woman that I had to have some tall cottonwoods along the river for my book, and to our surprise the old woman told her that there once were very tall cottonwoods exactly where I wanted them! That, furthermore, there was a cave near them, which I also had to have. The old woman said that highway construction had destroyed the cave and the cottonwoods due to age had been cut down. So then I knew I was working in wakan territory. Futhermore, Bill Lemons, who had once taught at the Standing Rock Reservation, knew a woman named Angela Fiske. She was the wife of Frank Fiske, government photographer. She was a pureblood Yankton Dakota. She was raised, not by her mother (who'd died) but by her gramma, Gramma Smoke. Gramma Smoke was a little girl when Lewis & Clark came through here in 1805-6. Gramma Smoke didn't see a white man until she was much older. So Angela's head was filled with pure Indian lore and myth. I interviewed her many times just before I began Conquering Horse. With all that hot in my head, I just rolled into the book. It came out slowly at first but almost always pure. And it started to go faster and faster.

Manfred once described Conquering Horse as a novel "that flies," meaning that it seemed directed by its own spirit, finding form with little urging, guiding its own becoming and being. Manfred had little difficulty getting the novel published, but the publishing history includes an intriguing footnote of interest to collectors.

While researching the first editions of the novels, the authors discovered that there were two quite different covers for Conquering Horse. One had a cloth cover which was about half blue and half red. On the spine, in addition to the title and author, was the publisher's name as Obolensky and McDowell. The second hardcover was black paper impressed to resemble cloth. On the spine of this cover, only Obolensky's name appears. All internal, textual material is identical. The dust jackets are also identical in all respects.

When shown the two books during August, 1979, Manfred was incredulous. He first concluded that the one with a black cover was fraudulent. Reflecting on McDowell, who was the primary editor for Conquering Horse as well as several other novels, Manfred recalled that there was a falling out between the Obolensky firm and McDowell about the time that Conquering Horse was published. He concluded that the two versions of the hardback cover for the same edition must have been related to McDowell's departure from Obolensky.

A telephone call to David McDowell confirmed Manfred's hypothesis. Shortly before Conquering Horse was published he left the publishing firm. The firm had only six months after he left to use his name on the book cover. Of the first edition impression of 7,500 copies, 5,000 copies were bound in the blue and red cover. As is customary with many publishers, not all copies were bound at once. When 2,500 copies were later bound, after McDowell had left, a new cover was required; therefore the black cover without his name on the spine. When asked why the dust jackets were identical for both versions, McDowell replied that in the publishing business more dust jackets are printed than books initially bound since dust jackets are especially expensive to rerun. All 7,500 dust jackets and printed texts were run at once and there were two separate bindings in two distinct covers. Interestingly, neither Manfred nor McDowell had ever seen the copy with the black cover.

b. Conquering Horse. New York: Pocket Books, Cardinal, 1960 [paperback: GC-90]. 331 pages.
Price: 50¢.

The cover illustration depicts an Indian man standing with a white fur robe draped loosely about him. At his feet sits a young Indian woman in a deerskin dress. Across the center of the cover is a wilderness scene of a stream, trees, and mountains rising to a yellow sky. In top brown border: CONQUERING HORSE [white letters]. At center: Frederick Manfred [black letters] / Author of LORD GRIZZLY / and RIDERS OF JUDGMENT [red letters]. In bottom brown border: The gripping story of a young Indian warrior who / stakes his life and his manhood on a dangerous pilgrimage. Left hand margin is a band of gold which has from top: Cardinal emblem with price, 50¢ / GIANT / CARDINAL / EDITION / GC-90 / THE / COMPLETE / BOOK. Back of cover has blurb on novel.

First printing, August, 1960.

c. Conquering Horse. New York: New American Library, Signet, 1965 [paperback: Y5492]. 277 pages. Price: $1.25.

The cover illustration depicts a naked Indian standing on a bluff and staring into the distance against a pink sky. Upper right has: SIGNET / . / 451-Y5492 / . / $1.25 / Signet emblem. In white letters shaded by black the cover reads from top: FREDERICK MANFRED / CONQUERING / HORSE. In black letters: A superb novel, by the author of LORD GRIZZLY. Spine has Signet emblem, identifying numbers, title, and author. Back has a blurb on the novel and on Manfred.
First printing, February, 1965.

A12 ARROW OF LOVE 1961

a. FREDERICK MANFRED / a black arrow / ARROW / OF LOVE / a black arrow / ALAN SWALLOW / DENVER.

(21.5 x 14 cm), 110 leaves, pp. [1] - [7], [8] - 220.

Contents: [1] ARROW OF LOVE; [2] list of last twelve books by author including this one; [note: an extra leaf of glossy paper is glued in here on 90 copies with a notice of special inscribed edition which reads as follows:]
>OF THIS SPECIAL EDITION
>OF ONLY NINETY COPIES
>OF ARROW OF LOVE
>MADE FOR THE FRIENDS
>OF FREDERICK F. MANFRED
>THIS IS COPY NUMBER
>INSCRIBED FOR

[3] title page; [4] Copyright (1961) and other publisher's matter; [5] quotation from J.F. Powers; [6] blank; [7] Contents; [8] - 220 text.

No identification of first edition.

Cover: Common stock red paper on pressed boards. The paper has small pink rectangles in irregular patterns. Spine has a glued-on

Original Books

label, cream colored and measuring approximately 10.5 x 1.5 centimeters, that identifies the book as: ARROW OF LOVE MANFRED [vertically in red letters].

Dust jacket: Jacket design includes spine. Against a white background several black teepees, a farmhouse, and another building are superimposed upon a woodcut image of red leaves and buildings. At top of jacket: FREDERICK MANFRED [red letters] / ARROW OF [black letters] / LOVE [red letters]. Spine has title and author vertically. Back of jacket lists under the heading, OTHER BOOKS AVAILABLE BY FREDERICK MANFRED, Morning Red, The Chokecherry Tree, Boy Almighty, and The Golden Bowl with brief blurbs on each. Publisher's name and address is at bottom. Front flap gives blurb on Manfred and Arrow of Love. Back flap continues blurb and gives publisher's address at bottom. The jacket was designed by Lowell Naeve, identified on paperback edition but not here.

Published October, 1961 in an impression of 750 copies of which 500 were bound in cloth. Of the 500, 90 were specially signed and numbered.
Price: $3.75.

Story notes: the three novelettes that comprise Arrow of Love were previously unpublished and were drawn from Manfred's files.

"ARROW OF LOVE / a romance;" pp. [9] - 69, text begins on 11.
Dedication, p. [9]: To Alan Swallow.
Place and date of composition: At Wrâlda
     May 1957
     Also May, 1961.

"LEW AND LUANNE / a comedy;" pp. [71] - 145, text begins on p. 73. Dedication, p. [71]: To Robert Penn Warren.
Place and date of composition: At Wrâlda
     September, 1952-November, 1953.

"COUNTRY LOVE / a pastoral;" pp. [147] - 220. Text begins on 149.
Dedication, p. [147]: To Waring Jones.
Place and date of composition: At Wrâlda
     September-October, 1948.

b. Arrow of Love. Denver: Alan Swallow, 1961 [paperback]. Price: $1.85.

This paperback edition is identical in all respects to the cloth edition by Alan Swallow except for the exclusion of the inscription leaf. The cover is the same in design but includes the following variants. Front of cover includes: SWALLOW PAPERBOOKS $1.85. Back of cover attributes cover design to Lowell Naeve, and includes a notice on Wanderlust, but excludes the notice on Boy Almighty and The Golden Bowl.

Of the 750 first impression copies, 250 were bound in paper.

A13 WANDERLUST 1962

a. Wanderlust / a trilogy / The Primitive / The Brother / The Giant [the three titles are to the right of a 3 cm. vertical rule] / Frederick Manfred / Alan Swallow / 1 cm. vertical rule / Denver, 1962.

(21.5 x 14 cm), 365 leaves, pp. [i] - [ii], [1] - [9], 10 -728, [729] - [730].

Contents: [i] WANDERLUST / A TRILOGY; [ii] list of last ten works by author including this one but excluding individual volumes of World's Wanderer; [1] Title page; [2] Copyright page (1962), and other publisher's matter; [3] Dedication: For Helen and James and Robert; [4] Note on the World's Wanderer Trilogy; [5] Program [notes on format]; [6] blank; [7] Rume I / The Primitive; [8] blank; [9] Part One / UPROOTING; 10-727 text; 728 ABOUT THE AUTHOR; [729]-[730] blank.

No identification of first edition.

Cover: Tan cloth on pressed boards. Front and back are blank. Spine: WANDERLUST / FREDERICK MANFRED / ALAN SWALLOW [all letters in black].

Dust jacket: Entire jacket is cream colored. Front of jacket alternates "Wanderlust" in red letters and "Frederick Manfred" in green letters. Title and author are repeated six times. Wanderlust shrinks in letter size from top to bottom. Frederick Manfred increases in letter size from top to bottom. The Spine duplicates front of jacket but with eight repetitions of title and author. Alan Swallow at bottom in red. Back of jacket has blurbs under heading: WHAT THE CRITICS SAID ABOUT WANDERLUST. Front flap gives price in upper right, $9.95, and a note from Alan Swallow on Manfred and his work follows. Back flap lists other books by Manfred available from Swallow. A brief blurb accompanies each title. Publisher's address at bottom.

Place of composition: revised from World's Wanderer at Wrâlda and Blue Mound.

Published January, 1962 in an impression of 500 copies.
Price: $9.95.

Notes: Several sources provide accounts of the writing of Wanderlust. Perhaps the fullest and most accurate account is in Conversations with Manfred, pp. 159-167. Further notes may be found in the narrative interview at the conclusion of this bibliography. It is an important story in the author's development as a writer and in his publishing history.

The plan for the unified work became clear to Manfred before he began writing the individual volumes of the early trilogy. He felt that Doubleday had rushed him too quickly on the trilogy, and that he didn't have the time he needed at that stage of his career to hone and refine the prose. Although much of the plot development of the trilogy depends heavily on a picaresque pattern and seriatim adventures, Manfred had developed a thematic view in which the young protagonist looks for meaning in religion, in economic theory and social problems, in scientism or technological materialism, and finally finds his meaning in "the expression of a beauty that he finds within himself" (Conversations, p. 167). The motif that carries the quest is music, particularly since Manfred designed the work after Beethoven's Third Symphony. In the work music is viewed in much the same way as Pater in The Renaissance, that is, as the highest achievement of artistic expression and manifestation of Beauty.

These themes were clear to Manfred at the writing of World's Wanderer, and he would have preferred them worked out in one volume. At the publisher's insistence World's Wanderer was published before the trilogy was finished in first draft (a common enough practice with long works at the time--consider USA by Dos Passos or Studs Lonigan by Farrell in America, and Tolkien's The Fellowship of the Ring in England). It is fair to say that Manfred lost control of his work, and that he knew this from the start.

It was while Manfred was finishing Morning Red in 1955 that he began to think again of the trilogy and of possibly paring it down to one new book. The process began by crossing out a few words from each page and gained steam from there. By 1957 Manfred set to work on it in earnest to construct a new draft. The process was more than simply trimming 1,280 pages to 727 pages. Wanderlust is tighter and trimmer in concept and plot as well. Manfred credits the stylistic tightening to his work on the Buckskin Man novels which demanded a crisper style. Also, many of the names in the trilogy, particularly those influenced by Frisian words, were changed or Americanized in Wanderlust.

A13 WINTER COUNT 1966

a. Winter Count / Poems   1934-1965 / by / FREDERICK MANFRED / emblem / James D. Thueson / Minneapolis / MCMLXVI.

(23.5 x 13 cm), 40 leaves, pp. [1]-[10], 11-78, [79]-[80].

Contents: [1] blank; [2] list of last thirteen books by author including this one; [3] WINTER COUNT; [4] pen and ink portrait (reversed) of Manfred by Duane Noblett; [5] title page; [6] Copyright (1963, 1966) and other publisher's matter, attribution of pen and ink portrait to Duane Noblett and book design to Barbara J. Bohach; [7] Dedication: To Uncle Clarence and Aunt Kathryn; [8] blank; [9] Contents; [10] blank; 11-78 text; [79] printing specifications; [80] blank.

Identification of first edition on p. [79].

Cover: Brown cloth on pressed boards, endleaves are green. Black shelfback. Front cover has author's signature in gold letters in upper center. Spine: MANFRED / WINTER COUNT [vertically in gold letters]. Back is blank.

Place of Composition: each poem identified individually in text.

Original Books 53

Published in an impression of 1,000 copies, of which 250 were autographed and numbered.
Price: $4.00
 $10.00 for inscribed edition.

Note: The paper in this edition is laid; watermark: Hamilton Kilmory.

b. WINTER COUNT. Berkeley, CA: Thorp Springs Press, [1977] [paperback].

Cover: High gloss tan paper. Front: WINTER COUNT / Frederick Manfred [red letters]. Spine: WINTER COUNT / The Poems / Frederick Manfred / Thorp Springs Press [vertically].
Price: $3.00.

Notes: Copyright pages reads:
 First Edition 1965 [sic]
 Second Edition 1977

and gives publisher's address as:
 Thorp Springs Press
 2311-C Woolsey
 Berkeley, California 94705

As of this writing, the present correct address for the publisher is:
 3414 Robinson Road
 Austin, Texas 78722.

The poetry of this volume centers around the title poem "Winter Count." It was an Indian custom to make hieroglyphic entries on an animal hide for each winter, counting the calendar year by winters. The hieroglyphs would evoke some memorable event of that year. While examining one such hide, Manfred determined to make a "winter count" for his life. Since much of his early artistic endeavor was in poetry, the form of the work fell naturally into this form. It should be noted also that this volume represents only a very small portion of the poetry that Manfred has written but has not submitted for publication. He has several files of such poetry.

A14 SCARLET PLUME 1964

a. Scarlet Plume / rule / FREDERICK MANFRED / Trident Press / rule / NEW YORK / 1964.

(21 x 14 cm), 192 leaves, pp. [i]-[xiv], [1]-365, [366]-[370].

Contents: [i]-[ii] blank; [iii] SCARLET PLUME; [iv] list of last eleven books by Manfred including this one but excluding the individual volumes of the World's Wanderer trilogy; [v] Title page; [vi] Copyright (1964) and other publisher's matter; [vii] Dedication:

Dear David McDowell--
  The import of this book may seem
shocking to some people--still it is a book
written in love, since it has always been
my belief that if one wishes to speak with
truth in the brain one must speak with love
in the heart.

  My friend, if I have achieved this, I
offer it all to you.
            Frederick

[viii] blank; [ix] Program of The BUCKSKIN MAN Tales; [x] quotation from General Henry R. Sibley, Letters to His Wife; [xi] Contents; [xii] blank; [xiii] SCARLET PLUME; [xiv] blank; [1]-365 text; [366] blank; [367] ABOUT THE AUTHOR; [368]-[370] blank.

No identification of first edition.

Cover: Tan cloth on pressed boards. Front and back blank. Spine: Scarlet / Plume / Frederick / Manfred / a red feather / Trident Press [all letters in green].

Dust Jacket: Jacket design includes spine. Against a brown background, shaded to resemble stained wood, jacket illustration depicts the head of an Indian man wearing a scarlet feather and the head of a blond woman. The two figures are highlighted by yellow shading. About them, at the bottom of jacket, ride

Indians on horseback. To the right, in background, settlement houses are burning. Artist's signature is in lower right as: Marchetti. At the top: Scarlet / Plume [white letters] / a novel by / FREDERICK MANFRED / author of Lord Grizzly [yellow letters]. Spine has title, author, Trident emblem, and publisher. Back has a full page photo of Manfred by Donald Ross and a brief biographical blurb at top in red letters. Front flap gives price in upper right, $4.95, and blurb on novel. Rear flap continues blurb and attributes jacket painting to Louis Marchetti and photograph to Ronald Ross.

Place of Composition: February 29, 1964
                              Blue Mound
                              Luverne, Minnesota

Published November 1964 in an impression of 5,000 copies. Three printings followed in impressions of 3,000 each, each of which is identified on the copyright page. Although there were no further hardcover printings, some copies exist that have no identification on the copyright page of impression number. Price: $4.95.

b. Scarlet Plume. New York: Pocket Books, Cardinal, 1966 [paperback: 75129]. 328 pages.
Price: 75¢.

Cover design depicts the back of a Sioux brave wearing a breech clout who is looking on a white woman in a deerskin dress. At top in a white rectangle: Scarlet Plume / FREDERICK MANFRED / Author of LORD GRIZZLY / The passionate love of a frontier-woman / for the savage Sioux who captured her. Upper left gives Pocket Book emblem, the numbers 75129, and price.
Published April, 1966.

c. Pluma Escarlata. Trans. Fernando Corripio. Barcelona: Bruguera, 1966. 319 pages. No price given.

Cover: Red cloth on pressed boards. Front has a crown shaped colophon in gold. Back is blank. Spine: Frederick / Manfred / PLUMA ESCARLATA / Bruguera [gold letters].

Dust jacket has a white background and depicts on front an

Indian with one feather holding a blond woman. In background are some armed warriors on ponies. Writing as follows: Un amor primitivo y salvaje / como la epoca que lo vio nacer./ Un relato de fuerza, pasion y violencia incontenibles. Back of jacket has a photo of Manfred and a blurb telling of the 1862 Indian Uprising, on which this novel is based. Flaps contain some information on Judith of the novel, Scarlet Plume and the 1862 Uprising.

d. Scarlet Plume. New York: New American Library, Signet. 1973 [paperback Y5567]. 317 pages. Price $1.25.

Cover design by Len McCance depicts an Indian man and a white woman in a canoe. The man is bare-chested, wearing a black and white feather in his hair, and blowing a birch horn. The woman is blond, wearing a black coat with white fur collar. The color tones are subdued blues and greens misting in the background of trees beyond the water. Upper right has: Signet · 451-Y5567 · $1.25 and Signet emblem. In white letters edged with black the cover reads: FREDERICK MANFRED / Scarlet / Plume. In black letters: The brutally realistic saga of the 1862 / Sioux Uprising, and the love of a pioneer white / woman for a savage red man. Spine has identifying numbers, publisher, title, author. Back has blurbs on Manfred and the novel.

First printing, August, 1973.

A15 THE MAN WHO LOOKED LIKE THE PRINCE OF WALES 1965

a. the / man / who / looked / like / the / prince / of / wales [because of the lengthy title, information normally found on the title page is found on the facing page (iv) reading as: FREDERICK MANFRED / Trident emblem / Trident Press / NEW YORK 1965].

(20 x 13 cm), 56 leaves, pp. [i]-[viii], [1]-178, [179] - [184].

Contents: [i] title vertically; [ii] blank; [iii] list of last fifteen books by author including this one; [iv] title page information; [v] title page; [vi] Copyright (1964) and other publisher's matter, design attributed to Patricia de Groot; [vii] Dedication: to / Vardis

/ Fisher; [viii] blank; [1] -178 text; [179]-[180] ABOUT THE AUTHOR: [181]-[184] blank.

No identification of first edition.

Cover: Brown cloth on pressed boards. Front and back blank. Spine: the / man / who / looked / like / the / prince / of / wales [yellow letters] / by / frederick / manfred [red letters] / trident / press [blue letters].

Dust Jacket: The background color of jacket is brown. Down the right hand side of front is the title in white letters followed by: A SHORT NOVEL BY / FREDERICK / MANFRED [red letters]. On lower left of front a man in black silhouette stands before an old fashioned mirror which is blue, framed in black. Spine gives title, author, and publisher. Back has photo of Manfred with blurb on author. Front flap gives price in upper right, $3.95, and blurb on novel. Back flap continues blurb and attributes jacket design to Lawrence Ratzkin. An outline of cover portrait is located at the bottom of rear flap.

Place of composition: April - October, 1963
                            Blue Mound
                            Luverne, Minnesota

Published September, 1965 in one impression of 5,000 copies. Price: $3.95.

Notes: The novel was completely drafted during Manfred's stay at the Huntington Hartford Foundation in the spring of 1963 and 1964. The foundation has an artist's colony of sixteen studio-cabins and invites artists worldwide in sculpturing, painting, writing, and music.
    The novel includes the first appearance in book form of Manfred's autobiographical character Alfred "Free" Alfredson. Notes on the background for the novel may be found in Conversations (pp. 31-32) and in the narrative interview at the conclusion of this study.

b. The Secret Place. New York: Pocket Books, 1967
[paperback 75190]. 176 pages.
Price: 75¢.

Cover: Against a mustard colored background, illustration at center depicts the heads of a man and a woman. From top, cover reads as: The / Secret / Place [maroon letters] / "An / earthy / rendition of / Main Street / America" / the New York Times Book Review [black letters] / Frederick / Manfred [green letters]. Original title noted at bottom. Upper left corner has kangeroo emblem of Pocket Books, numbers 75190, and price, 75¢. Back cover has blurb and an illustration of a man and woman standing in a field of grain.

First printing, January, 1967.

Note: Should the novel be reissued in paperback, Manfred intends to restore the original title.

A17 KING OF SPADES 1966

a. KING OF SPADES / spade device from playing card / FREDERICK MANFRED / Trident emblem / TRIDENT PRESS, NEW YORK / 1966.

(21 x 14 cm), 160 leaves, pp. [i] - [xiv], 1-304, [305] - [306].

Contents: [i] KING OF SPADES; [ii] list of last fourteen books by author including this one [note: the list includes Wanderlust but excludes the individual volumes of World's Wanderer]; [iii] title page; [iv] Copyright (1966), and other publisher's matter; [v] Dedication: To Alan C. Collins, / trusted friend; [vi] blank; [vii] Epigraph: The Creator made the people-- / come and see them. / -- Indian Prayer; [viii] blank; [ix] Program / of / THE BUCKSKIN MAN TALES; [x] blank; [xi] Contents; [xii] blank; [xiii] KING OF SPADES; [xiv] blank; 1-304 text; [305] ABOUT THE AUTHOR; [306] blank.

No identification of first edition.

Cover: Gray cloth on pressed boards. Front and back blank. Spine: MANFRED [vertically] / spade device from playing card / King / of / Spades [white letters] / spade from playing card / TRIDENT PRESS [vertically].

Dust jacket: Against a black background, across the top in large

Original Books 59

red-orange letters: KING / OF / SPADES [a blue ornament is on each side of "OF"]. At Bottom: A NEW NOVEL [blue letters] / BY FREDERICK MANFRED [orange letters] / AUTHOR OF [blue letters] / LORD GRIZZLY AND SCARLET PLUME [blue letters]. Spine: MANFRED [blue letters vertically] / KING OF SPADES [orange letters vertically] / Trident emblem in blue / TRIDENT / PRESS [blue letters]. Back of jacket has a photo of Manfred and biographical information same as on p. [305]. Front flap gives price in upper right, $5.95, and blurb follows. Back flap continues blurb and attributes jacket design to Robert Geissmann.

Published in 1966 in an impression of 5,000 copies.
Price: $5.95.

Place and date of composition: Blue Mound
           Luverne, Minnesota
           January 6, 1966

Notes: King of Spades, in Manfred's estimation, contains some of his best writing. The book was written rapidly but was initially delayed by the writing of The Man Who Looked Like the Prince of Wales. In 1963 Manfred was awarded a fellowship at the Huntington Hartford Foundation and planned to use the time to write King of Spades. Instead the story of The Man Who Looked Like The Prince of Wales came to him and he wrote that novel rapidly over the time of the foundation grant, actually drafting in the story in a space of approximately three weeks. He started King of Spades in the spring of 1964, again at the Huntington Hartford Foundation.

b. King of Spades. New York: Pocket Books, Cardinal, 1968 [paperback: 75272]. 258 pages.
Price: 75¢

The cover design depicts the parlour of a bordello in which a cowboy stands between two women clad in negligees and striped stockings. Above them, in a gold oval frame, and against an orange background: King / of Spades / Frederick Manfred / AUTHOR OF / LORD GRIZZLY and SCARLET PLUME / A stark and unforgettable / novel about one of mankind's / strongest and oldest / taboos . . . . At upper left: Pocket Books Kangeroo emblem, numbers 75272, and price, 75¢. Back has oval frame of front cover enlarged. Inside the frame is a quotation from the novel and illustration of a man and woman.

First printing, May, 1968, identified on copyright page.

c. King of Spades. New York: New American Library, Signet, 1973 [paperback: 451-Y5630]. 254 pages. Price: $1.25.

Cover design depicts a man in buckskin holding a rifle and standing in foreground. To the man's left stands a woman in a blue dress with a black patch over her right eye. To the man's right stands a man in a black suit and black hat. They stand in a field against a light blue sky. At top in black-edged white letters: FREDERICK MANFRED / KING / OF SPADES. In black letters at center: A magnificent novel of the American West / by the author of LORD GRIZZLY. Back cover depicts an adobe house and has a blurb on Manfred and the novel.

First printing, October, 1973, identified on copyright page.

A18 APPLES OF PARADISE AND OTHER STORIES 1968

a. APPLES OF PARADISE / and other stories / FREDERICK MANFRED / emblem used to mark book divisions / TRIDENT PRESS / NEW YORK / Trident Emblem.

(21 x 14.5 cm), 144 leaves, pp. [1]-[9], 11-285, [286]-[288].

Contents: [1] APPLES OF PARADISE / and Other Stories; [2] list of last fifteen works by author including this one but excluding the individual volumes of World's Wanderer; [3] title page; [4] Copyright (1945, 1950, 1965, 1966, 1967, 1968), Acknowledgment to journals in which stories first appeared, other publisher's matter; [5] Contents; [6] blank; [7] -285 text; [286] blank; [287] ABOUT THE AUTHOR; [288] blank.

No identification of first edition.

Cover: Black cloth on pressed boards. Front and back blank. Spine: Frederick Manfred / Apples of Paradise / Trident Press [vertically in green letters].

Dust jacket: Front and spine are in black. At the top of front, in white script letters: Apples of / Paradise / and Other Stories / by Frederick Manfred. Lower part of front jacket has a small (12.5 x 3 centimeter) drawing of a green field, black mountains, and a white and orange sky. Spine has author, title, and publisher vertically in white letters. Back of jacket provides biographical information on author same as on p. [287]. Front flap gives price, $5.95, in lower right and blurb. Back flap continues blurb and attributes jacket design to James and Ruth McCrea.

Place of composition is listed individually after each story.

Published March, 1968 in an impression of 4,108 copies (figure confirmed by Simon and Schuster].
Price: $5.95.

Story Note:
"The Mink Coat" pp. [7]-64, text begins on [9].
Dedication, p. [7]: To Keith D. Kennedy
Place and date of composition: Blue Mound
          Luverne, Minnesota
          March, 1966
          Also November, 1967

"Apples of Paradise," pp. [65]-98, text begins on [67].
Dedication, p. [65]: to Debby [note: "Debby" refers to Professor John De Bie]".

Place and date of composition: Huntington Hartford Foundation
          and Blue Mound
          June and November, 1963.

"Wild Land," pp. [99]-137, text begins on [101].
Dedication, p. [99]: to David Hubbard Smith
Place and date of composition: At Wrâlda
          Bloomington, Minnesota
          June, 1957
Previously published: Plainsong, I (Winter, 1967), pp. 23-52.

"Blood Will Tell," pp. [139]-158, text begins on [141].
Dedication, p. [139]: to Harold Aardema

Place and date of composition: At Wrâlda
                                Bloomington, Minnesota
                                December, 1954
Previous published: Loci (Winter, 1965), pp. 48-63. Note: Loci was a student literary journal of Calvin College which appeared twice yearly. It has since been replaced by Dialogue which appears six times a year. The winter, 1965 Loci contained a special alumni section to which Manfred contributed this story.

"Goodhearted Man," pp. [159]-181, text begins on [161].
Dedication, p. [159]: to Alan McIntosh
Place and date of composition: At Wrâlda
                                Bloomington, Minnesota
                                December, 1953
Previously published: The Minnesota Review, VI (1966), pp. 103-120.

"Treehouse," pp. [183]-212, text begins on [185].
Dedication, p. [183]: to John K. Sherman
Place and date of composition: At Wrâlda
                                Bloomington, Minnesota
                                June, 1951
Previously published: Plainsong, I (Winter, 1963), pp. 19-42.

"High Tenor," pp. [213]-232, text begins on [215].
Dedication, p. [213]: To Tom
Place and date of composition: At Wrâlda
                                Bloomington, Minnesota
                                February, 1951

"Boys Will Be Boys," pp. [233]-251, text begins on [235].
Dedication, p. [233]: to Aubrey McEachern
Place and date of composition: At Wrâlda
                                Bloomington, Minnesota
                                December, 1946
Previously published: The Minnesota Review, V (January-April, 1965), pp. 25-35.

"Footsteps in the Alfalfa," pp. [253]-285, text begins on [255].
Dedication, p. [253]; to Uncle Hank

Original Books 63

Place and date of composition: 609 Ontario Street, S.E.
Minneapolis
June - August, 1939
Previously published:
1) "Footsteps in the Alfalfa" [shorter version], Esquire, XXIV (September, 1945), pp. 76-77, 141-145.
2) "Omen of Spring" [Section 2 of "Footsteps in the Alfalfa"], Minnesota Quarterly (Winter, 1950), pp. 4-13.
3) "Maitiids Teken" [Translation into Frisian of "Omen of Spring"], trans. Marten Sikkema, de Tsjerne, V (January-February, 1950), pp. 47-56.
Note: "Footsteps in the Alfalfa" is excerpted from the first two drafts of This is the Year.

A19 EDEN PRAIRIE 1968

a. Eden Prairie / rule / FREDERICK MANFRED / Trident emblem / Trident Press New York.

(21 x 14 cm), 176 leaves, pp. [i]-[ii], [1]-[8], 9-348, [349]-[350].

Contents: [i] Eden Prairie; [ii] list of last sixteen books by author including this one, but excluding the individual volumes of World's Wanderer; [1] title page; [2] Copyright (1968) and other publisher's matter; [3] Dedication: TO / John R. Milton / friend; [4] Acknowledgment: To the directors of the Avon Foundation go my sincere / thanks for a fellowship to help me write this book. / FREDERICK MANFRED; [5] Contents; [6] blank; [7] Eden Prairie; [8] blank; 9-348 text; [349] ABOUT THE AUTHOR; [350] blank.

No identification of first edition.

Cover: Mustard colored cloth on pressed boards. Front and back blank. Spine: Eden Prairie / Frederick Manfred [vertically] / Trident Press [vertically].

Dust jacket: jacket design includes spine. On right half of front stand the pillars and small section of a board porch of an early American farmhouse. The porch roof is shingled with green hexagonal shingles. A pot of red geraniums stands on the porch. To the left of porch, at bottom of front jacket runs a green band with grass blades depicted. Moving up, a thin band of white and a thin band of gray cloud. The upper two-thirds depicts a solid black cloud with a tornado funnel touching down to the grass. From top, in white letters: Eden Prairie / A NOVEL BY / Frederick Manfred. Spine: Eden Praire [vertically] / a red horizontal rule / Frederick Manfred / Trident Press. Back of jacket has same biographical paragraphs as page [349]. Front flap has price in lower right, $6.95, and blurbs on Manfred and on the book. Back flap continues blurb and attributes jacket design to James and Ruth McCrea.

Place of composition: September 16, 1967
       Blue Mound
       Luverne, Minnesota

Published September, 1968, in one impression of 1,355 copies [figure confirmed by Simon & Schuster].
Price: $6.95.

Note: Eden Prairie was accepted immediately for publication.

A20 CONVERSATIONS WITH FREDERICK MANFRED 1974

a. Conversations / with Frederick / Manfred / Moderated by John R. Milton / with a Foreword by Wallace Stegner / The University of Utah Press Salt Lake City.

(22.9 x 14 cm), 94 leaves, pp. [i]-[vii], viii-xiii, [xiv]-[xvii], xviii, 1-169, [170], [note: pages are numbered only on recto as 2/3, etc.].

Contents: [i] Conversations / with Frederick / Manfred; [ii] pen and ink drawing and identification of drawings by Arnold John Dyson; [iii] title page; [iv] Copyright (1974) and other publisher's matter; [v] Contents; [vi] list of last twenty works by Manfred not including this one, and Milk of Wolves, as "To Be Released"; [vii] drawing; viii-ix publisher's preface; x-[xvi] Foreword by Wallace Stegner; [xvii] photo of Manfred by John Dziadecki;

Original Books 65

xviii Conversations . . . ; 1-[170] text. Drawings by Arnold John Dyson appear on pages [ii], [vii], 6, 44, 48, 72, 98, 106, 120, 154.

No identification of first edition.

Cover: Brown paper. Front duplicates type of title page with pen and ink drawing of lizard as on p. [ii]. Spine has title vertically. Rear is blank.

Place of Composition: Transcribed from thirteen video tapes made in the studio of KUSD-TV at the University of South Dakota, Vermillion, South Dakota, in early 1964. Six tapes were made the first day, four on the second, and three on the third day of taping.

Published in 1974 in an impression of 3,000 copies.
Price: $5.00.

Note: Manfred edited the transcript of the tapes and interpolated material by footnotes. The verso of rear endleaf gives printing specifications on book.

A21 THE MANLY-HEARTED WOMAN 1975

a. The / Manly- / Hearted / Woman / by Frederick Manfred / Crown Publishers, Inc., New York.

(23 x 15 cm), 96 leaves, [i] - vi, 1-185, [186].

Contents: [i] The / Manly- / Hearted / Woman; [ii] list of last 22 works by Manfred including this one and Milk of Wolves as 1975 [sic]; [iii] Title Page; [iv] Copyright (1975) and other publisher's matter, book design attributed to Ruth Smerechniak; [v] Dedication: FOR MY FRIENDS / William Everett Lemons, Jr. / and Max Roger Westbrook; vi Glossary of Indian terms used in book; 1-185 text; [186] blank.

Note: The Manly-Hearted Woman precedes Milk of Wolves in this bibliography to harmonize the printed dates of publication in the texts. MOW was in fact composed and published before MHW. The latter was delayed from the fall of 1975 to the spring of

1976 for release, although it was already bound with the 1975 date.

No identification of first edition.

Cover: Beige paper on pressed boards. Orange cloth shelfback. Front and back blank. Spine: THE MANLY-HEARTED WOMAN / FREDERICK MANFRED [vertically in black letters] / 523744 / Crown.

Dust Jacket: Jacket design includes spine. Design depicts an Indian woman in buckskin holding a spear and standing against orange fields. The sky varies in color from yellow at lower center to tan at top. At the top in black letters: "Not many novelists can match Manfred's powers as a storyteller / in small as well as great matters"--The New York Times / FREDERICK MANFRED [in blue letters] / THE MANLY- / HEARTED / WOMAN [in red letters] / A spirit from the clouds / told her to live as a man . . . . / Her heart told her to / live as a woman. Spine: THE MANLY-HEARTED WOMAN / FREDERICK MANFRED [vertically] / Crown. Rear Cover: A 19 x 14 centimeter photo of Manfred by Bruce M. Buursma. Front flap has price at upper right, $7.95, blurb follows. Rear flap continues blurb. One paragraph of biographical data. Attributes jacket illustration to Richard Lomonaco. Publisher's address at bottom.

Place of Composition: Blue Mound
                              Luverne, Minnesota

Published in an impression of 4,145 copies. A second impression, unidentified, of 3,050 copies followed [figures confirmed by Crown].
Price: $7.95.

Notes: The germ of the story was planted one day in 1973 when Manfred was talking with William E. Lemons at the University of South Dakota who had lived with Indians for a time and was attracted to their lore. Lemons pointed out an episode in David Lavender's Dent Fort about an Indian lad named Flat Warclub. Later, Lemons gave Manfred a brief article on a society of Indian women called The Manly-Hearted. Following the discussion Manfred taught his class in creative writing (the last class of the year).

During the long drive back to Luverne he mulled the story over in his mind. By the time he arrived at Luverne nearly the entire plot was outlined on a clipboard that Manfred had next to him on the seat of his car. Within two weeks the story was fully sketched out and the first draft was written over the summer of 1973.

The ms. was rejected twice. David McDowell of Crown Publishers accepted the ms. on a first reading.

b. The Manly-Hearted Woman. New York: New American Library, Signet, 1977 [paperback E 7648]. 204 pages. Price: $1.75.

The cover design of this paperback edition includes spine. In the foreground an Indian woman in buckskin holds a war lance. A brave watches from behind right. Mountains rise in the distance to a blue sky. From the top, cover reads: ACCLAIMED AUTHOR OF LORD GRIZZLY / FREDERICK MANFRED / THE / MANLY- / HEARTED / WOMAN / A NATIVE AMERICAN SAGA OF VIOLENCE, SEXUALITY, / COURAGE, AND LOVE . . . "STRANGE AND HAUNTING . . . WE ARE TOTALLY EN-CLOSED IN AN INDIAN WORLD." / -- NEW YORK TIMES. Back cover contains blurb. Published simultaneously in Canada by General Publishing Company Limited.

A22 MILK OF WOLVES 1976

a. a novel by / FREDERICK MANFRED / MILK OF WOLVES / Avenue Victor Hugo / Boston 1976.

(28 x 21.7 cm), 127 leaves, [i] - [iv], 1-250. Pages are divided by a vertical rule with two full length columns per page.

Contents: [i] Title Page: [ii] Left column, Dedication: This work is for my friends: ROBERT BLY and JAMES WRIGHT. In the center of the left column an appreciation: to the directors of the Louis W. and Maud Hill Family Foundation and to the English Department of the University of South Dakota. At bottom: Copyright (1976). Right column: List of last 22 books by author including this one listed as: MILK OF WOLVES -- duology. [iii] BOOK ONE / VILLAIN IN THE CITIES / pen and ink illustration similar to cover illustration / MILK OF WOLVES; [iv] blank; 1-250 text.

Identification of first edition on back cover.

Cover: Paper in white. Cover illustration in tones of light brown by Thomas Barber depicts a sculptor with hammer and chisel, and a woman sculpted from waist up out of block of marble located behind. At top: MILK OF WOLVES / a novel [black letters]. At bottom: by [black letters] / FREDERICK MANFRED [light brown letters]. Spine: MILK OF WOLVES / · / MANFRED / / AVH [vertically]. Back: on left column, photo of Manfred, one paragraph blurb on book, identification of cover illustration by Thomas Barber, price $6.95. Right column, under heading, About the Author, biographical data. Bottom carries note of special edition as follows:

MILK OF WOLVES will be available in a special sewn cloth bound version of this First edition, signed by the author. Only three hundred copies will be made. The price per copy is $20. (postage and handling included). Orders will be accepted immediately for delivery in October, 1976, in time for Christmas giving.

Publisher's address follows.
Note: This special edition was never published. See notes on novel below.

Place of Composition: Blue Mound
        Luverne, Minnesota
Published in an impression of 2,000 copies.
Price: $6.95.

Notes: In the story of Juhl Melander of Milk of Wolves Manfred has provided his fullest representation of his artistic vision. As such it is an important book in his corpus. Yet, it is also perhaps the one with the most battle-scarred publishing history.
 Milk of Wolves was written approximately during 1967-1968. The rough-typed draft (from longhand script) was finished in August, 1969. The final draft was typed late in 1969. The work involved the same painstaking research and personal experience that marked Lord Grizzly, including a stay with a hermit in

Original Books

northern Minnesota in order to learn "how a man fends for himself alone, what you do, what kind of a house you have, how you make it, what your routines are, what kind of food you eat, where you get it, when do you get the mail, do you chop a lot of wood, what kind if heat do you have, what's your entertainment, do you have a radio." (from an interview with Manfred, Calvin College Chimes, November 14, 1969, p. 4). In Manfred's estimation: "I wanted to have it look as if it were inevitable, as if I were writing my own autobiography, as if it couldn't be any other way" (Chimes, November 14, 1969, p. 4).

This intensely personal rendition met with little favor with publishers. In all it was rejected nearly thirty times. In the following notes, excerpts from rejections are printed to give some indication of attitudes regarding the work. The excerpts are representative of those received and are addressed either to Manfred or his agent. Some comments are valuable for their critical observations and these are reproduced more fully.

> PUBLISHER ONE: . . . A book the length of this current project offers no prospect for the publisher other than more red ink. Its projected length and Fred's high hopes require, and I mean the word literally, a belle-lettristic trade house willing to wait for Fred's ultimate place in American literature. We have gone as far as we possibly can." [The publisher had reviewed only the first third of the rough draft.]

> PUBLISHER TWO: [summarized from a phone call] "I don't like your boarish Juhl. I fear that your notion of an artist is different from mine. I had hoped that you'd present the artist as a sensitive gentle, very understanding, kindly person . . . Juhl is far too heartless with women. Though I will say that MILK OF WOLVES contains some of the best writing I've seen you do. It upsets me very much to have to say no. It's the toughest decision I've had to make in my whole publishing career."

> PUBLISHER THREE: "Juhl is simply not that interesting or empathic a character for me, and as a result I couldn't sustain my interest in either his artistic or amatory travails . . . . You've worked hard and long on this, you are a writer of stature, and you deserve to prosper."

PUBLISHER FOUR: "I don't have to tell you that he is a professional writer, his credits speak for themselves, and here he has written a big old-fashioned novel. It seems to have a lot of fat in it and would, I think, need a great deal of cutting in order to be publishable."

PUBLISHER SIX: "What was I doing making the proposal in the first place about our house becoming your publisher? A casual thing? Whistling in the dark? Etc.? No, not at all; it was of course made in perfectly good faith. The hard facts are that since then we have ended a fiscal year and have turned to royalty accounting, etc. We are damn short of money. I cannot feel right in taking on the Manfred publications right now . . . ."

PUBLISHER NINE: "That's quite a saga you have woven in MILK OF WOLVES! I've read every word of it, and there have been other readings of it too. We all agree that the writing is vivid and flowing, that you create backgrounds and settings magnificently. Juhl is an old-fashioned superhero, and his story is of the old-fashioned grand adventure romance genre, too. And this alas is the reason why it isn't our kind of fiction, and we'd have a problem reaching the right audience for it."

PUBLISHER TEN: "I don't see it attracting the largely urban reader today in quantities sufficient to at least break even, much less make a few dollars for author and publisher over and above costs. Your LORD GRIZZLY and CONQUERING HORSE, my two favorites, captured two great myths of mountain man and Indian in such convincing and engrossing fashion as to become narrative classics. Each caught the poetic truth, the animating dream, that lies behind the factual recitation. But I don't see where MILK OF WOLVES, despite its length, evokes anything nearly as majestic as the earlier two novels. The absorbing book-length narratives today all compete with movies and television, usually losing out."

PUBLISHER ELEVEN: "I felt that there were fatal drawbacks to Juhl's character that didn't permit me to either like him or believe him. Truthfully, I'm not sure which it is;

Original Books 71

there are limitations to Juhl that I can't be sure you intend. For example, in the end Juhl decides that his life was 'wonderful,' but I get the feeling that he is mistaken and that it is only a final reaffirmation that thinks he is wonderful. The 'bad' has never really penetrated his own egoism and was only capable of producing a rather surface 'sadness.' Also, the 'bad' never seemed to outweigh his extraordinary good luck."

The manuscript eventually landed with the small Boston press of Avenue Victor Hugo. Their promise to produce three hundred cloth bound, signed copies was well-intentioned, but the plates were seriously damaged by a firm that did the actual printing and the financial return on the novel had been too slim to warrant resetting the entire plates. Thus the cloth bound edition never appeared.

A23 GREEN EARTH 1977

a. GREEN EARTH / a novel by Frederick Manfred / Emblem / Who can see the green earth anymore / as she was by the sources of Time? / --Matthew Arnold / Crown Publishers, Inc. New York.

(22.6 x 15 cm), 348 leaves, pp. [i] - [viii], ix - x, [xi] - [xii], 1-721, [722] - [724].

Contents: [i] - [ii] blank; [iii] GREEN EARTH; [iv] blank; [v] list of last twenty-three books by author including this one; [viii] Copyright (1973, 1977) and other publisher's matter including attribution of book design to Rhea Braunstein; ix-x Preface; [xi] BOOK ONE / Lady of the House / Emblem [used to mark book divisions] / Dedication: To / ALICE / mother / January 3, 1891; April 19, 1929; [xii] blank; 1-721 text; [722] - [724] blank.

No identification of first edition. Second impression is identified as "Second Printing" on copyright page and on dust jacket.

Cover: Light blue paper boards. Blue shelfback in cloth. Front and back blank. Spine: GREEN EARTH / FREDERICK MANFRED [vertically in gold letters]. Bottom of spine has numbers: 529858 / CROWN.

Dust Jacket: Front depicts a colonial plaque against the white of dust jacket. The plaque varies in color from green at bottom to blue at center and to violet at top. Top two-thirds of plaque has GREEN EARTH in white letters in type face of title page. In center of cover in black letters: A NOVEL BY / FREDERICK MANFRED. Bottom third has outline of a farmhouse against a windmill against a cloud, centered. At lower left, in small black script letters running vertically, is artist's signature: J. Sposato. Spine has title in white letters and author in black letters running vertically in a colonial plaque of same colors as front. Back cover has six review blurbs under heading: CRITICAL ACCLAIM FOR THE MANLY-HEARTED WOMAN. Bottom right has ISBN: 0-517-529858. Front flap has price in upper right: $10.00. Blurb follows and continues to rear flap. One paragraph of biographical data on rear flap, attribution of jacket design to John Sposato and publisher's address.

Place of Composition: Blue Mound
        Luverne, Minnesota

Published September, 1977 in an impression of 7,317 copies. A second impression of 5,249 copies followed, identified as "Second Printing." [impression figures confirmed by Crown].
Price: $10.00.

Notes: Green Earth is in many respects Manfred's earliest work. It is a novel of rediscovery, of going home. Like Thomas Wolf, in his work if not the title of his most famous novel, Manfred believes that all art is a process of "going home again." Art begins in the real stuff of one's life experience. The green earth is not only the story of the land, it is the fertile soil from which springs the "really real," as young Free of this novel describes it, of the artistic vision. The really real roots in one's personal life experience.

  In an interview with James W. Lee (<u>Studies in the Novel</u>, 5, Fall, 1973, pp. 358-382), Manfred reported: "I have a book written which comes to some 1,300 pages . . . . It starts with the life of my father and mother before I am born. I had hoped to get that in about fifty pages, but it turns out that it took me 320 pages . . . . And then I have another 700 pages describing my babyhood and the babyhood of my brothers until I am seventeen." In its final draft the ms. of <u>Green Earth</u> came to 1,607 pages.

Green Earth was also a releasing ground for some of Manfred's earliest notebooks. In a sense, Manfred had already begun discovering his novelistic roots in a short story called "Harvest Scene" published in the Calvin College Chimes (March 2, 1933) while he was a student at Calvin College. His western home had a steady call for him for several reasons. One such reason was recounted by Manfred in a newspaper article: "I was in college and lonesome for my mother, who had just died. I began to write things I remembered about her in the back of my college notebooks. That became the core or germ of this book" ("Author says writing a 'chancy' life," Sioux City Journal, October 26, 1978). Altogether, these early notes for the novel amounted to some 142 pages. The novel was often on his mind in following years. In an unpublished letter dated June 5, 1947, Manfred wrote of a work called "A Son of the Road" which was to become Green Earth.

Why this lengthy delay? Manfred suggested an answer: "I decided I wouldn't write this book until I got older and more mature, in the middle years, so I wouldn't get any anger or venom in it" (Sioux City Journal, October 26, 1978). Part of the critical discontent with the early World's Wanderer Trilogy clearly centered on this issue. The Trilogy slashes widely at assorted targets. Green Earth is a work of emotional maturity. The novel was systematically begun on March 30, 1970 when Manfred wrote the first two pages in a ledger. The writing was set aside during the summer of 1973 while Manfred wrote the first draft of Manly-Hearted Woman.

After reading Manfred's description of Green Earth in his interviews with John R. Milton (Conversations with Manfred), David McDowell of Crown Publishers asked to see the book. Manfred sent him the 1,607 page manuscript in April, 1976. In mid-September McDowell called to report: "I read your novella." Manfred reflects on McDowell's comment: "I knew two things right away. First he liked it. Second, it was too long." McDowell thought that the book was too long, but also a bit repetitious due to the notes over many years that had gone into the work. Manfred decided he could trim it by cutting two lines from every page (on a basis of 24 lines per page). He wound up cutting eight lines per page prior to publication.

A24 THE WIND BLOWS FREE 1979

a. A REMINISCENCE BY FREDERICK MANFRED / rule / The Wind Blows Free [special lettering] / pen and ink drawing of a tree in the wind / rule / THE CENTER FOR WESTERN STUDIES / Augustana College / Sioux Falls, South Dakota / 1979.

(21 x 13.5 cm), 133 leaves; pp. [i]-[xiii], I-VI, [VII], [1]-[2], 3-255, [256].

Contents: [i]-[ii] blank; [iii] THE WIND BLOWS FREE; [iv] list of last twenty-four books by Manfred including this one; [v] title page; [vi] Copyright (1979) and other publisher's matter, attribution of illustrations to Elsie Thorson; [vii] Dedication: For my sweet children / FREYA, MARYA, AND FREDERICK; and acknowledgment ["To DWAYNE O. ANDREAS / who helped out when I was in need. / Also / In memory of ROBERT SMITH SURTEES]; [viii] blank; [ix] photo of Manfred at age 18 on farm at Doon, Iowa, August, 1930; [x] Graduation photo of Manfred, 1934; [xi] photo of Manfred in writing cabin at Luverne, by James Studio; [xii] blank; [xiii] Poem by Manfred entitled SPECIAL FACE, written Spring, 1934, at Calvin College; I-VI Foreword by Manfred; [VII] blank; [1] THE WIND BLOWS FREE; [2] blank; 3-255 text; [256] blank. Pen and ink illustrations by Elsie Thorson are on pages 30, 80, 125, 151, 183.

Identification of first edition on copyright page [vi].

Cover: Brown cloth on pressed boards. Front and back are blank. Spine: THE WIND BLOWS FREE / Frederick Manfred / Emblem / The Center for Western Studies [in yellow letters].

Dust jacket: Entire dust jacket is beige. Second color in brown-gold depicts hills of The Badlands. At top, in special black lettering, is title. At right center, in black script letters, a poem by Manfred also in the text of the book. At bottom in brown-gold letters: FREDERICK MANFRED. Back has a photo of Manfred in cabin at Luverne by James Studio, same as p. [xi] of book, and biographical blurb. Front flap gives blurb on book and attributes illustrations to Elsie Thorson. Back flap continues blurb and has three paragraphs on The Center for Western Studies at bottom.

Place of composition: Roundwind
       Luverne, Minnesota

Original Books   75

Published September, 1979, in an impression of 3,425 copies [figure confirmed by Center for Western Studies].
Price: $9.95.

Notes: The reminiscence was completed by summer, 1978. The story of the book is the famous Miss Minerva Baxter story which Manfred told at "Jim's" party in Minneapolis and which, in Manfred's judgment, convinced him he had found his voice as a novelist--that of a storyteller. After telling the story he worked straight through typing some fifty pages of manuscript by afternoon of the following day. Manfred considered the material for inclusion in The Golden Bowl, but excised this more openly biographical account as the early novel changed shape.
  Crown Publishers originally considered the work, but after publishing Green Earth decided they wanted to publish Manfred's novel Sons of Adam next. Crown kept The Wind Blows Free for nearly a year. Increasingly, Manfred felt the works should be published in the order in which they were written; therefore he asked Crown if he could submit the book elsewhere. Crown agreed to let him submit it to The Center for Western Studies which quickly consented to publish the work.
  The Center for Western Studies specially bound 10 copies of The Wind Blows Free in leather. These volumes were sold for $75.00 each.

A25 SONS OF ADAM 1980

a. SONS / OF / ADAM / rule / A Novel by / FREDERICK / MANFRED / A HERBERT MICHELMAN BOOK / CROWN PUBLISHERS, INC. / NEW YORK.

(22.6 x 15 cm), 176 leaves, pp. [1] - [viii], 1-341, [342] - [344].

Contents: [i] SONS OF ADAM: [ii] list of last 25 books by author including this one; [iii] Title page; [iv] Copyright (1980) and other publisher's matter including attribution of book design to Camilla Filancia and identification of first edition; [v] Dedication: To / WARING JONES / Acknowledgment to National Endowment for the Arts for financial assistance / Also in remembrance of / CHARLES MONTAGU DOUGHTY; [vi] blank; [vii] SONS OF ADAM; [viii] blank; 1-341 Text; [342] - [344] blank.

Identification of first edition on Copyright page [iv].

Cover: Light green paper boards. Off-white shelfback in cloth. Front and back blank. Spine: Manfred / rule / SONS / OF / ADAM / rule / CROWN.

Dust Jacket: Jacket design includes spine. On front, against black background and in white letters: A novel by / Frederick Manfred / SONS / OF / ADAM. Cover illustration on lower half has a portrait of two men against a green semi-circle framed by a red border. One man, dressed in shirt, tie, and vest, holds a pencil; the other is in boxing trunks and gloves. Across bottom of cover is a portrait of fields and a farmhouse. Spine of jacket has author, title, and publisher. Back of jacket has critical blurbs on Manfred and ISBN. Front flap has price, $12.95, upper right, title, author, and blurb on book. Back flap has a photo of Manfred by Larry Risser, a brief blurb on Manfred, attributes jacket design to Lydia Rosier, and has publisher's address at bottom.

Section B: Other Works

I. Student Writings

During Manfred's years at Calvin College (1930-34), he published extensively in the College literary outlets, the yearbook Prism and the student newspaper Chimes. During the year 1933/34 Manfred was an associate editor of Chimes. At the time Chimes was the major literary outlet on the campus and regularly carried poetry and short fiction. Occasionally it carried special issues of creative work. These issues later evolved into the College literary magazines Loci (1950's through 60's) and Dialogue (1970's).

The significance of the student writings in Manfred's case cannot be discounted. Early notes and pages drafted during his student days later found their way into Green Earth. Some of the prose writings of this period clearly contain the germ of later stories. Several of the works are signed "F.F.".

The following checklists are arranged chronologically.

1931

B1 "Breath of Neumenon," [poem], Chimes (May 22, 1931), p. 3.
B2 "A Violin" [poem], Chimes (November 19, 1931), p. 3.
B3 "Rain and Sunshine" [poem], Chimes (November 19, 1931), p. 3.

1932

B4 "To a Leaf" [poem], Chimes (January 14, 1932), p. 3.
B5 "Thunder-Clouds" [poem], Chimes (March 17, 1932), p. 3.
B6 "A Day" [poem] Prism (May, 1932). p. 102.
B7 "A Tender Memory" [poem], Chimes (October 6, 1932), p. 4.
B8 "A Western Picture" [descriptive prose essay], Chimes (October 6, 1932), pp. 4-5.
B9 "Thoughts" [poem], Chimes (October 20, 1932), p. 5.
B10 "The Hour-Glass" [poem], Chimes (December 15, 1932), p. 2.
B11 "Christmas Eve" [poem], Chimes (December 15, 1932), p. 6.

1933

B12 "A Harvest Scene" [short story], Chimes (March 2, 1933), p. 5.
B13 "O Beauty, Why?" [poem], Chimes (May 12, 1933), p. 4.
B14 "An Echo" [poem], Prism (May, 1933), p. 33.
B15 "A Plea" [poem], Prism (May, 1933), p. 33.
B16 "O Beauty, Why?" [poem], Prism (May, 1933), p. 33.
B17 "A Question of Culture" [editorial], Chimes (September 22, 1933), p. 2.
B18 "Death Comes at Midnight" [short story], Chimes (November 2, 1933), pp. 4-7.
B19 "Varieties of Canine Experience: A Book Review of Virginia Woolf's Flush" [essay-review under column headed 'Feike Peeks into Literature"], Chimes (December 14, 1933), p. 10.

1934

B20 "Critical Attitude" [editorial], Chimes (February 8, 1934), p. 7
B21 "O Dramatists; Where Art Thou?" [editorial], Chimes (April 12, 1934), p. 9.
B22 "Broken Prism" [short story], Chimes (April 12, 1934), pp. 13-16.
B23 "The West Sends A Call' [poem], Prism (May, 1934), p. 79.
B24 "Sonnet" [poem], Prism (May, 1934), p. 91.
B25 "A Moment of Peace" [poem], Chimes (October, 1934), p. 18.

II Short Stories

B26 "Child Delinquent," Northwest Life, XXVII (March, 1944), pp. 26-27.
B27 "Horse Touch," Northwest Life, XVIII (May, 1945), pp. 18-20.
B28 "Footsteps In The Alfalfa," Esquire XXIV (September, 1945) pp. 76-77, 141-145.

Other Works 79

B29 "Omen of Spring," Minnesota Quarterly (Winter, 1950), pp. 4-13.
B30 Same. "Maitiids Teken," trans. Marten Sikkema [into Frisian], de Tsjerne, V (January-February, 1950), pp. 47-56.
B31 "Where the Grass Grows Greenest," The Farmer, LXXI (June 6, 1953), pp. 14-15, 32-33; (June 20, 1953) pp. 10, 25.
B32 "Lord Grizzly," [condensed version], Real, V (December 1954), pp. 12-13, 48-63.
B33 "Judith: A Fragment," Plainsong, II (Winter, 1962), pp. 4-10.
B34 "Blood Will Tell," Loci (Winter, 1965), pp. 48-63.
B35 "Boys Will Be Boys," The Minnesota Review, V (January-April, 1965), pp. 25-35.
B36 "Good-Hearted Man," The Minnesota Review, VI (1966), pp. 103-120.
B37 "Wild Land," Plainsong, I No. 1 (Winter, 1967), pp. 25-52.
B38 "Tree House," Plainsong, I, No. 3 (1967), pp. 19-42.
B39 "The Voice of the Turtle," South Dakota Review, XI (Autumn, 1973), pp. 89-105.
B40 "Sleeping Dogs," Fiction (1975), pp. 17-23.
B41 "The Founding of Rock River Church," collected in The Far Side of the Storm, ed. Gary Elder. Los Cerrillos, NM: San Marcos Press, 1975, pp. 92-113.
B42 "Splinters," Dakota Arts Quarterly, 1 (Summer, 1977), pp. 12-15.
B43 "Hijinks with the Minister's Son," collected in 25 Minnesota Writers Minneapolis: The Nodin Press, 1979.
B44 "Free," Dialogue (December, 1979), pp. 30-31.

III. Poems

B45 "Touch and Go," Plainsong, II (Summer, 1962), p. 41.
B46 "Winter Count," The South Dakota Review, I (December, 1963), pp. 21-32.
B47 "Touch and Go" [expanded version], Plainsong, I, No. 1 (Winter, 1967), p. 9.

B48 "My Coffee is Cold," Dacotah Territory (Winter-Spring, 1973), p. 13.
B49 "My Other Lives," Dacotah Territory (Winter-Spring, 1973), p. 13.
B50 "Lily Susan," New Letters, XLI (Spring, 1975), pp. 21-32.
B51 "Frisian Love," Studio One (Spring, 1976), pp. 42-43.
B52 "Amelia Sound Asleep," Studio One (Spring, 1977), p. 30.
B53 "Act Your Age," Poets of Southwestern Minnesota. Ed. Joe and Nancy Paddock. (January, 1978), pp. 39-43.
B54 "Winter Count," reprinted in Growing Up In Iowa. Ed. Clarence Andrews. Ames: Iowa State University Press, 1978, pp. 66-79.
B55 "Where is Everybody," Madog, II, No. 2 (1979), pp. 91-92.

IV. Articles and Published Letters

The following checklist does not include Manfred's work as a reporter. While working for the Prospect Park, New Jersey Prospector in 1936, Manfred wrote a regular column amounting to some thirteen entries under the heading "The World Around Us." From 1937 to 1939 Manfred wrote for the Minneapolis Journal as a sports reporter and general reporter. For a time he wrote a series of columns under the heading "North Side." Further, while hospitalized at Oak Terrace, Minnesota, Manfred contributed two essays to the Sanatorium Terrace Topics in 1941: "In Defense of Women" and "Independence--Do We Lose It Under Stringent Laws?" During 1942 Manfred joined the editorial staff of Modern Medicine in Minneapolis.

B56 "Report from Minnesota," New Republic, CIX (October 11, 1943), pp. 480-481.
B57 "Little Innovation?" [letter], The Saturday Review, XXXII (March 12, 1949), pp. 19-20.
B58 "Author Nicks Self on Edge of Own Wit," Chicago Sun Times (March 8, 1950), Sec. II, p. 6.
B59 "In Memoriam Address (On the Occasion of the Burial of Sinclair Lewis' Ashes in Sauk Centre, Minnesota, January 28, 1951)," Sauk Centre Herald, LXXXIII (February 1, 1951), pp. 2, 5.
B60 Same, The Minneapolis Labor Review, XLIV (February 15, 1951), p. 3.

Other Works

B61 Same [excerpt], New York Times (January 29, 1959), p. 19.
B62 "Sinclair Lewis: A Portrait," The American Scholar, XXIII (Spring, 1954), pp. 162-184.
B63 "The Evolution of a Name," Names, II (1954), pp. 106-108.
B64 " ' Censorship' Can Hit Bible, Manfred Says," Minneapolis Sunday Tribune (April 10, 1955), p. 1.
B65 "Wanted: More Ornery Cusses," Chicago Sunday Tribune (December 4, 1955), Book Section, p. 24.
B66 "Speaking of Books" [Guest Column], The New York Times Book Review (February 12, 1956), p. 2.
B67 "Manfred Tells about Characters" [letter], Minneapolis Sunday Tribune (December 16, 1956), Open Forum Section, p. 3.
B68 "Children of the Motherland," Saturday Review, XLIII (June 4, 1960), p. 31.
B69 "A Definition of 'The Educated Man,' " Minnesota Journal of Education, XLI (April, 1961), p. 12.
B70 "Backgrounds for Western Writing," The Denver Westerners Monthly Roundup, XVI (August, 1961), pp. 4-11.
B71 "Mark Shorer and Sinclair Lewis," Plainsong, II (Summer, 1962), pp. 47-50.
B72 "Some Notes on Sinclair Lewis' Funeral," The Minnesota Review, III (Fall, 1962) pp. 87-90.
B73 "Letter to The Journal" [letter], The Reformed Journal, XII (May-June, 1963), p. 24.
B74 "The Western Novel--A Symposium: Frederick Manfred," The South Dakota Review, II (Autumn, 1964), pp. 7-9.
B75 "Mother East Could Learn from West," Minneapolis Tribune (December 15, 1965), Entertainment and Arts Section, pp. 1, 4.
B76 "Letter to Names" [letter], Names, XIV (December, 1966), pp. 247-248.
B77 "The Novelists of Western America," Chicago Daily News (January 7, 1967), Panorama Section, p. 8.
B78 "Alan Swallow: Poet and Publisher," Denver Quarterly (1967), pp. 27-31.

B79 "A Real Challenge for Army Engineers," St. Paul Sunday Pioneer Press (May 14, 1972), p. 2.
B80 "For Homegrown Culture," [for an advertisement by Northwestern National Bank], Minneapolis Tribune (August 20, 1972), Sec. A, p. 19.
B81 "On Being a Western American Writer," Hennepin County History, XXXI (Fall, 1972), pp. 14-17.
B82 "The Valley," The Minnesota Volunteer, XXXVI (March, 1973), pp. 44-48.
B83 "The Minnesota River Valley," The Minnesota Volunteer XXXVI (May-June, 1973) pp. 44-48.
B84 "On Being a Writer in the Midwest," Publishers Weekly (October 22, 1973), p. 78.
B85 "Artist as a True Child of God," The South Dakota Review, XI (Winter, 1973-1974), pp. 44-50.
B86 "Writing in the West" [Cassette Tape, No. 1107], Deland, Florida: Everett/Edwards, Inc., 1974.
B87 "Introduction" to Wind Without Rain by Herbert Krause. Sioux Falls: Brevet Press, Inc., 1975, pp. 9-10.
B88 "Flesh Compass" [Guest Word Column], New York Times Book Review, (January 12, 1975).
B89 "Ives and Faulkner," introduction to Student Musicologists at Minnesota, ed., Johannes Riedel, VI (1975-1976), pp. 1-4.
B90 "Frisians Living In Siouxland?" Sioux Falls Argus Leader (July 15, 1976), Sec. C, p. 12.
B91 "Mandala: Walking Against Earth's Turning," Eastwest, VII (June, 1977), pp. 22-23.
B92 "Hubert Horatio Humphrey: A Memoir by Frederick Manfred," Minnesota History (Fall, 1978), pp. 86-101.
B93 "Ninety is Enough: A Portrait of My Father," The Iowa Review, X, No. 2 (Spring, 1979), pp. 1-21.

V. Reviews
B94 Portrait of an Artist with 26 Horses by William Eastlake, Chicago Daily News (April 20, 1963), Panorama Section, p. 11.
B95 Mountain Man by Vardis Fisher, Western American Literature, VI (Spring, 1966).

Other Works 83

B96 Sweet Medicine by Peter J. Powell. Chicago Daily News (April 11, 1970), p. 10.
B97 Derleth on Schorer and Staying at Home by August Derleth. Minneapolis Tribune (January 24, 1971), Sec. E, p. 4.
B98 Faulkner: A Biography by Joseph Blotner. Minneapolis Tribune (March 24, 1974). Sec. D, p. 10.
B99 How It Was by Mary Welsh Hemingway. Minneapolis Tribune (October 3, 1976), Sec. D, p. 12.
B100 Selected Letters of William Faulkner, ed., Joseph Blotner. Minneapolis Tribune (February 6, 1977), Sec. D, p. 12.
B101 A Place To Come To by Robert Penn Warren. Minneapolis Tribune (March 27, 1977), Sec. D, p. 14.
B102 Selected Poems: 1923-1975 by Robert Penn Warren. Minneapolis Tribune (March 27, 1977), Sec. D, p. 14.
B103 Growing up in Minnesota by Chester G. Anderson. Moon and Lions Tailes, II (1977), pp. 97-98.
B104 Words and Savages by Ronald Robinson and Arthur Huseboe. Minneapolis Tribune (February 26, 1978).

VI. Interviews

In addition to Conversations with Manfred, entered in this bibliography under Original Books, Manfred has participated in several interviews. Customarily these are collected under secondary works. The scholarly value and the author's reflections on his own literature and contemporary literature would seem to make inclusion under primary works obligatory in this case. In this section interviews and symposia are listed in chronological order. Many newspaper articles are in an interview-essay format, and these are noted as such and included in Section C.

B105 "West of the Mississippi: An Interview with Frederick Manfred," Critique, II (Winter, 1959), pp. 35-56. [This interview was conducted on July 13, 1958 at Manfred's residence outside Minneapolis.]
B106 "The Western Novel--A Symposium," The South Dakota Review, II (Autumn, 1964), pp. 7-9.

B107 "Interview," Collage (Spring, 1969), pp. 21-28. [Collage is a publication of Worthington State Junior College, Minnesota. Manfred has expressed some dissatisfaction with the transcription from tapes.]

B108 "Interview with Frederick Manfred," with Stephen Sieberson, Calvin College Chimes. The interview was published in two parts: "The Inner-directed Manfred," Chimes (November 14, 1969), p. 4; "Manfred Apart from Society," Chimes (November 21, 1969), p. 3.

109 "Interview with Frederick Manfred," with John R. Milton, The South Dakota Review, VII (Winter, 1969-70), pp. 110-130. [This interview is reproduced, for the most part, in Conversations with Manfred.]

B110 "Frederick Manfred Talks About Sinclair Lewis," Sinclair Lewis Newsletter, II (Spring, 1970), pp. 1-5.

B111 "An Interview in Minnesota with Frederick Manfred," with James W. Lee, Studies in the Novel, V (Fall, 1973) pp. 358-382). [The interview was conducted at Manfred's home in Luverne, May 5-7, 1973.]

B112 "Milton, Manfred and McGrath: A Conversation on Literature and Place," with Thomas McGrath, Dacotah Territory (Fall-Winter, 1974-75), pp. 19-26.

B113 "The Writer's Sense of Place," The South Dakota Review, XIII (Autumn, 1975), pp. 5-6. [In this Special Issue writers were asked to respond to eight questions in symposium fashion.]

B114 "Frederick Manfred," with John R. Milton, Fiction, IX (1976), pp. 16-19, 61. Conversations with Frank Waters. Ed. John R. Milton. Chicago: Swallow Press, 1971, pp. 77-86. [In Chapter Seven John Milton interviews Frank Waters and Manfred.]

Section C: Critical Studies of Manfred's Work

The critical bibliography is divided into three sections. The first consists of scholarly, critical studies which focus primarily on Manfred's work. The second section consists of a checklist of other works on Manfred including newspaper and magazine articles, brief accounts in journals, critical studies which consider Manfred's work in part, and miscellanea. The third section lists Master's Theses and Doctoral Dissertations on Manfred's work.

I. Critical Articles and Books, Annotated

Many of the entries that follow are annotated as to subject matter or theoretical content. Whenever possible, a direct statement of thesis from the article is quoted. In other cases a brief sypnopsis is offered. Some entries were unavailable or published too recently for annotation. In no case is this annotation, or the lack thereof, intended to pass judgment on the value of the article. Its use is informative only.

Andrews, Clarence A. A Literary History of Iowa. Iowa City: University of Iowa Press, 1972.

> Andrews considers Manfred's work through Winter Count (1966), and compares Manfred's work in theme and technique to other Iowan novelists. Andrews also provides a sypnopsis of critical opinion, with documentation, on the early novels. See particularly pp. 113-22.

Arthur, Anthony. "Manfred, Neihardt, and Hugh Glass: Variations on an American Epic, "Where the West Begins, Ed. Arthur R. Huseboe and William Geyer. Sioux Falls, SD: Center for Western Studies Press, 1978, pp. 99-109.

> Arthur states as his thesis that "Neihardt and Manfred chose to tell a story that fulfilled . . . the essential requirements of the epic: namely, that it offer a definition of the national character, through the depiction of a protagonist whose adventures illustrate and exemplify it," and the Hugh Glass story provides "valuable insights into both western American history and the literature that derives from it" Neihardt's Song of Hugh Glass and Manfred's

Lord Grizzly are compared on three points: the fight, the woman, the confrontation.

Austin, James C. "Legend, Myth and Symbol in Frederick Manfred's Lord Grizzly," Critique: Studies in Modern Fiction, VI (Winter, 1963-64), pp. 122-30.

Considering the thesis that Lord Grizzly was "Nourished in the author's feeling for the history and local color of his native region, and brought to fruition in rich allusion to our literary and mythical past," Austin explores the literary and mythical background to the work. The heroic stature of Hugh Glass is also allied with biblical analogues.

Bebeau, Donald. "A Search for Voice: A Sense of Place in The Golden Bowl," South Dakota Review, VII (Winter, 1969-70), pp. 79-86.

Bebeau examines The Golden Bowl as an odyssey, the story of a search or quest, and compares this to Manfred's quest for a place (Siouxland), and a voice (story-teller of Siouxland). In Bebeau's assessment, Manfred is a regionalist who nonetheless touches upon the universal in mankind.

De Boer, Peter P. "Frederick Feikema Manfred: Spiritual Naturalist," The Reformed Journal, XIII (April, 1963), pp. 19-23.

De Boer considers Manfred's discovery of "the spiritual in the natural," and focuses upon Manfred's concept of the nature of man. The thesis is explored from Boy Almighty. in which "man is an animal" but one capable of self-discipline, through Lord Grizzly, in which Hugh Glass has his "soul remade" by "the magic of the Badlands." Other works are considered. Manfred responded to the essay with a letter printed in The Reformed Journal, XIII, May-June, 1963, p. 24.

Flora, Joseph M. Frederick Manfred. Boise State University Western Writers Series. Boise, ID: Boise State University, 1974.

In this 52 page monograph Flora provides a critical introduction and survey of Manfred's work through Eden Prairie and Apples of Paradise (1968).

----------. "Frederick Manfred," in Dictionary of Literary Biography ("American Novelists Since World War II, Second Series"), Vol. 6. Ed. James E. Kibler, Jr. Detroit: Gale Research Company, 1980, pp. 201-207.

A biographical overview of Manfred's career with some critical assessment of the novels. Page 204 of the entry reproduces the revised typescript of page 11 from Sons of Adam. Entry includes a selected bibliography.

----------. "Siouxland Panorama: Frederick Manfred's Green Earth," Midwestern Miscellany (The Center for the Study of Midwestern Literature and Culture), VII (1979), pp. 56-63.

----------. The Works of Frederick Manfred. Cassette Tape, number 1120. Deland, Florida: Everett/Edwards, Inc., 1974.

Kellogg, George. Frederick Manfred: A Bibliography. Denver: Alan Swallow, 1965. Also printed in Twentieth Century Literature, XI (April, 1965), pp. 30-35.

Lyons, John O. The College Novel in America. Carbondale: Southern Illinois University Press, 1962.

Lyons briefly considers Thurs of The Primitive as a type of the rebel.

Meyer, Roy W. The Middle Western Farm Novel in the Twentieth Century. Lincoln: University of Nebraska Press, 1965.

Under an entry for Feike Feikema, Meyer discusses This is the Year (pp. 122-126).

Milton, John R. "The American Novel: The Search for Home, Tradition, and Identity," The Western Humanities Review, XVI (Spring, 1962), pp. 169-80.

----------. "Frederick Feikema Manfred," Western Review, XXII (Spring, 1958), pp. 181-99.

In a survey of the first eight novels including Riders of Judgment in a Post-Script, Milton explores the thesis that taken singly each novel deals with its own situations and sets of characters, but collectively these provide "The Long View of Man." The essay considers Manfred's technical and stylistic development as a novelist.

--------------------. "Lord Grizzly: Rhythm, Form and Meaning in the Western Novel," Western American Literature, 1 (Spring, 1966), pp. 6-14.

Milton provides a careful analysis of the structure and unfolding meaning of Lord Grizzly, allying Manfred's novel with traits typifying the western novel as a genre. Varying rhythmical patterns of the novel are established and considered with the narrative technique.

--------------------. "The Novel and the American West," South Dakota Review, II (Autumn, 1964), pp. 56-76.

The essay investigates the question of what makes the western novel western focusing on several novelists. Attention is paid to Manfred on pp. 71-73 with observations which are developed more fully in Milton's "Lord Grizzly: Rhythm, Form and Meaning in the Western Novel."

--------------------. "Voice from Siouxland: Frederick Feikema Manfred," College English, XIX (December, 1957), pp. 104-11.

In this relatively early essay, Milton accounts for the enduring significance of Manfred's work despite some unfavorable reviews from the eastern literary establishment. The essay explores the view expressed in The Golden Bowl that "Man's origins are 'holy' and man must endure" through the first eight novels, along with assessments of Manfred's developing style.

--------------------. "The Western Novel: Sources and Forms," Chicago Review, XVI (Summer, 1963), pp. 74-100.

The material here is essentially the same as in "The Novel and the American West." The material on Manfred is developed more fully in "Lord Grizzily: Rhythm, Form and Meaning in the Western Novel."

Oppewall, Peter. "The Greening of Frederick Manfred," The Reformed Journal, XXVIII (December, 1978), pp. 19-21.

In an essay-review of Green Earth, Oppewall explores two principal themes related to the earlier fiction: "the rigors and hardships of life on the farm" and Manfred's "own psychological and spiritual development" as an artist.

Oppewall, Peter. "Manfred and Calvin College," Where the West Begins. Ed. Arthur R. Huseboe and William Geyer. Sioux Falls, SD: Center for Western Studies Press, 1978, pp. 86-98.

Oppewall compares names, places, and events of The Primitive with the actual names, places, and events of Manfred's four years at Calvin College. The essay fully reveals the real event from which the fictional event arises. Further, the essay explores Manfred's relation to the religious views of his college community.

Roth, Russell. "The Inception of a Saga: Frederick Manfred's 'Buckskin Man,'" South Dakota Review, VII (Winter, 1969-70), pp. 87-99.

The unifying theme of the Buckskin Man Tales is "the search for the true self in a context of an evolving and generic American self." Roth explores backgrounds for the novel, tracing influences to D.H. Lawrence, William Carlos Williams, and William Faulkner, among others.

Swallow, Alan, "The Mavericks," Critique: Studies in Modern Fiction, II (Winter, 1959), pp. 74-92.

Swallow recounts the difficulties of western writers finding a place in the eastern publishing establishment and his personal involvement with several of these authors. Of importance here is his recollection of the publication of Morning Red.

----------. [Same] An Editor's Essays of Two Decades. Seattle and Denver: Experiment Press, 1962, pp. 353-357.

Timmerman, John. "As I Knew Them," Dialogue [A Calvin College journal of student and faculty opinion] (April, 1975), pp. 20-22.

A professor of English at Calvin College for over thirty years, Timmerman recalls his student days as a contemporary of novelists Manfred, Peter De Vries, David Cornel De Jong, and Meindert De Jong. Observations of Manfred's style and use of form are offered along with personal reflections on the novelist.

----------. "Siouxland and Suburbia," The Reformed Journal (October, 1959), pp. 9-11.

In an essay-review of Manfred's Conquering Horse along with Peter De Vries' The Tents of Wickedness (Published the same year, 1959), Timmerman explores the contrasting locales of the two works, in which there are "contrasting visions underlying and informing their depiction." The essay considers also the contrasting artistic styles of the authors.

Timmerman, John H. "Pursuit of a Vision: Notes on Frederick Manfred and His Publishing History," Dialogue (December, 1979), pp. 26-29.

The essay focuses on early, middle, and late periods of Manfred's career to reveal the author's pursuit of a literary vision.

Westbrook, Max. "The Ontological Critic," Rondez-Vouz: A Journal of Arts and Letters (Special Issue on Western American Literature), VII (Winter, 1972), pp. 49-66.

----------. "Riders of Judgment: An Exercise in Ontological Criticism," Western American Literature, XII (May, 1977), pp. 41-51.

Westbook offers eleven assertions about archetypal criticism and applies these in a reading of Riders of Judgment.

Wright, Robert C. Frederick Manfred. Boston: Twayne Publishers, Inc., 1979.

The format of the book follows the pattern of the Twayne Series on American authors. In addition to a biographical chapter, the book contains interpretive essays on Manfred's works. A final chapter discusses major themes and a postscript evaluates Manfred's status as an author. The work contains a selected bibliography and biographical chronology.

--------------------. "The Myth of the Isolated Self in Manfred's Siouxland Novels." Where the West Begins. Ed. Arthur R. Huseboe and William Geyer. Sioux Falls, SD: Center for Western Studies Press, 1978, pp. 110-118.

Borrowing the term "Myth of the Isolated Self" from Joyce Carol Oates, Wright uses the term here to explore the sense of separation which arises from rational categorization and the sense of unity which arises from intuitional knowledge. The latter is a mark of the early Siouxland novels. These novels demonstrate "the individual as an interlocking member with all living things."

Wylder. D.E. "Frederick Manfred: The Quest of the Independen Author." Books at Iowa, XXXI (November, 1979), pp. 16-31

--------------------. "Manfred's Indian Novel." South Dakota Review, VII (Winter, 1969-70), pp. 100-09.

Considering the fact that most novels about the American Indian "have as their major conflict the clash between the Indian society and the encroaching white, or Anglo, society," Wylder explores Manfred's Conquering Horse as the exception in that it deals solely with one Indian culture.

--------------------. "Recent Western Fiction." Journal of the West, XIX (January, 1980), pp. 62-70. Brief critical discussion of The Manly-Hearted Woman and Green Earth.

--------------------. "The Western Hero from a Strange Perspective." Rondez-Vouz: A Journal of Arts and Letters (Special Issue on Western American Literature), VII (Winter, 1972), pp. 23-30.

II. Checklist of News Reports and Miscellaneous Items

Although a sizeable body of scholarship has developed around Manfred's work, an invaluable source of information about the works, and particularly the early works, is located in brief notices and in newspaper accounts. The latter are particularly revealing. Since, in his early career at least, Manfred was considered something of a regionalist hero, these items do much to fill in the life of that region. Often based on reporters' interviews with Manfred, the articles also record the author's attitudes toward his work, his career, and his readership. This is particularly true of the "Siouxland" newspapers, which are often enlivened by interviews with local citizens and accounts of their reactions to their neighbor.

Because these accounts form a rather extensive list some pruning was necessary. For example, in this case press notices for the sale of a book were excluded. Other pieces of minimally relevant material were also excluded. But the value of the following entries, which are presented here as a checklist, is significant for Manfred scholarship. Also included here are book or journal entries in which Manfred is given brief notice. In many cases identifying or supplemental information is entered in brackets.

Aardema, Harold. "Doon Editor Gives Picture of Writer Manfred." Sioux City Journal (October 24, 1954), p. 10.

----------------. "Ink-Spots." Doon Press [Doon, Iowa] (December 17, 1977, pp. 1, 2 [Comparison of names and places in Green Earth to actual names and places].

----------------. "Thoughts on the 100th anniversary of the Bonnie Doon Railroad: Manfred shares his memories." Doon Press (February 15, 1979), pp. 1, 2.

Andrews, Clarence. "Frederick Manfred, Empire Builder." The Iowan (Summer, 1976), pp. 47-51.

"Author Manfred returns to Alma Mater." Calvin College Chimes (January 26, 1979), p. 1.

"Author Manfred Talks Freely; Comments on Artists and Calvin." Calvin College Chimes (February 27, 1959), p. 3.

"Author says writing a 'chancy' life." Sioux City Journal (October 26, 1978), Sec. A, p. 2 [includes photo].

"Author will Return to Alma Mater." Grand Rapids Press (February 6, 1972), Sec. A, p. 8.

Ballantine, Elizabeth. "A Son Not all in Doon Approve Of-- 'Famed' Author Fred Manfred." Des Moines Register (August 25, 1977), Sec. B, p. 1. Reprinted in the Doon Press (September 15, 1977), p. 10.

" ' Big Moose' Hitched to a Star." Grand Rapids Press (September 26, 1947) [includes photo].

Bjerk, Irid. "Manfred-Bjork [sic] trade big talk on farming in the good old days." Doon Press (July 6, 1978), p. 10 [includes photo of Manfred and his Grampa Feike (on stack), his father (pitching off), his uncle Herman Van Engen holding reins, and his brother Edward John in front of horses].

Butcher, Fanny. "The Literary Spotlight." Chicago Tribune (October 30, 1949), Sec. 4, p. 11.

Buursma, Bruce. "In Short, Manfred as the Big Man on Campus." Grand Rapids Press (February 20, 1972) [includes photo].

Daley, Dave. "Truth, Not Facts, Is Historical Novelist's Goal." Minneapolis Star (September 4, 1975), Sec. C. p. 2.

Des Moines Register (August, 1977). [People Section], Sec. B, p. 1 [includes photo].

Dienhart, Paul. "Storyteller of Siouxland," Co-op Country News [St. Paul, MN] (January 7, 1980), pp. 3, 13. [photos by Greg Ellis].

Dunn, Stephen, "Notes from a Writers Conference: To Frederick Manfred." South Dakota Review (Autumn, 1972), pp. 80-81 [a poem].

Flanagan, John T. "A Half-Century of Middle Western Fiction." Critique: Studies in Modern Fiction, II (Winter, 1959), pp. 22-23, 33.

"Fred Manfred recalls glorious days of beseballing [sic] in Doon." Doon Press (March 17, 1977), p. 11 [includes photo].

Frederick, John T. "The Farm in Iowa Fiction." Palimpsest, XXXII (March, 1951), pp. 121-152 [discusses This is the Year].

Fridsma, Bernard. "Frederick F. Manfred." De Strikel, IV (December, 1958), pp. 168-169.

----------------. "De Literatuer Fan Fryske Lanforhuzers Yn Amearika." De Tsjerne, V (Jan-Feb, 1950), pp. 27-36 [written in Frisian].

Gilbert, Harriet, "Feikema, The Giant Novelist." St. Paul Pioneer Press (November 12, 1950), p. 7.

Gray, James. "Compensations in Interruptions: Here's Witness." St. Paul Dispatch (May 24, 1939), p. 18.

Gruchow, Paul. "Frederick Manfred, writer." Worthington [MN] Daily Globe (September 5, 1979), Sec. B, pp. 1, 3 [includes photos by Joe Rossi].

Hall, James B. "Frederick Manfred" in Contemporary Novelists. Ed. James Vinson London, ST. James Press, 1972, pp. 826-828; New York: St. Martin's Press, 1976, pp. 883-886.

Hammond, Ruth. "Frederick Manfred Enjoys Living, Writing in Luverne." Minneapolis Tribune (January 6, 1979), Sec. B, pp. 1, 2 [includes photos].

Heilman, Robert B. "Versions of Documentary, Arts and Letters." Sewanee Review, LVI (Autumn, 1948), pp. 678-79 [discusses The Chokecherry Tree].

"Honor Among the Artists, or the Tale of Two Gestures." Editorial. Esquire, 23 (March, 1945), [p. 6].

Johnson, Ron. "Minnesota Profile." The Minnesota Motorist (October, 1968). p. 6.

Kellogg, George. "Hymn to Buckhood." Western Humanities Review, XVIII (Summer, 1964), p. 224 [a poem].

Kimball, Jim. " ' Big' Author Sizes Up People, Places." Minneapolis Tribune (July 23, 1967) pp. 1, 12.

Koerselman, Glada, "Doon's Ire has cooled off: Author Manfred Signs Book." Le Mars Daily Sentinel (September 20, 1979), Focus Section, p. 1 [photo by Dick Koerselman].

Kramer, Mary. "America's 'Heartland' is Just That in the Eyes of Novelist Manfred." Grand Rapids Press (February 11, 1979), Sec. F, p. 2 [interview-essay; includes photo].

LaBelle, Tom. "Feike's Home." Grand Rapids Press (February 13, 1965). p. 13 [photo].

McConagha, Al. "Manfred--Voice of Siouxland." Minneapolis Tribune (Ocotober 25, 1964), Entertainment and Arts Section, pp. 1, 4 [interview-essay; includes photo].

MacDonald, Helen, "Boy Almighty." Northwest Life, XVII (October, 1944). p. 19.

"Manfred Home." Doon Press (July 15, 1976), p. 2 [story of the house at Blue Mound State Park].

"Manfred Remembers a Lifetime in 'Siouxland' " Minneapolis Sunday Tribune (December 4, 1977), Sec. S, pp. 1, 8.

"Manfred Tells About Characters in His New Novel 'Morning Red,' " Minneapolis Sunday Tribune (December 16, 1956) Arts Section, p. 1.

Miller, Mark. "Siouxland Area Leads Nation in Creative Book Production." Sioux City Sunday Journal (December 4, 1960), Sec. C, P. 1.

Minnesota Writers: A Collection of Autobiographical Stories by Minnesota Prose Writers. Ed. Carmen N. Richards. Minneapolis: T.S. Dennison and Co., Inc., 1961, pp. 216-218.

Ode, Kim. "Staying alive keeps Manfred's material fresh." Sioux Falls Argus-Leader (September 6, 1979), Sec. C, p. 1 [includes photo of Manfred by John Danicic, Jr.].

Paulka, Frank. Iowa Authors: A Bio-Bibliography of Sixty Native Authors. Iowa City: Friends of the University of Iowa Libraries, 1967.

Rawson, Rosemary. "Fred Manfred Put 'Siouxland' On The Map, But He Sure Upsets Some Of His Godly Neighbors." People, IX (April 10, 1978), pp. 78, 81-82 [photos by Gerald R. Brimacombe].

Roth, Russell. "Is Manfred the Midwest's Faulkner?" Minneapolis Sunday Tribune (August 1, 1954), Feature Section, pp. 1, 6 [includes photo].

"Saluting Frederick Manfred." English Notes, XXI (February, 1975), pp. 8-9.

Schorer, Mark. Sinclair Lewis, an American Life. New York: McGraw-Hill, 1961, pp. 743-745, 808 [details a meeting between Manfred and Lewis].

Sherman, John K. "Meet Feike Feikema, Novelist." Minneapolis Tribune (September 28, 1944), p. 4.

Spavin, Don. "Troubles Gave Author His Start." St. Paul Sunday Pioneer Press (May 9, 1976), p. 7.

Steensma, Robert C. "The South Dakota Novel: Thoughts After a Centennial." North Dakota Quarterly, XXX (Spring, 1962), pp. 40-41.

Swallow, Alan. "Giant Frederick Manfred Has His Ups and Downs." The Denver Post (May 19, 1957), p. 10.

Swets, Robert. "Manfred Proclaims Artist True Child of God." Calvin College Chimes (February 18, 1973), p. 4 [includes photos].

Twentieth Century Authors, first supplement. Ed. Stanley Kunitz. New York: Wilson, 1955, pp. 633-635.

Warfel, Harry. American Novelists of Today. [New York: American Book Company, 1951], pp. 153-154.

Westbrook, Max. "Conservative, Liberal, and Western: Three Modes of American Realism." The South Dakota Review, IV (Summer, 1966), pp. 3-19.

----------------. "The Practical Spirit: Sacrality and the American West." Western American Literature, III (Fall, 1968), pp. 193-206.

Western American Literature." Chicago Daily News Panorama (January 28, 1967), p. 1.

Williams, John. "The 'Western': Definition of the Myth." Nation, CXCIII (November 18, 1961), pp. 400-04.

III. Dissertations and Theses

Boeveld, Bernice E. "A Study of the Depression Years through the Fiction of Frederick Feikema Manfred." Master's Thesis, University of Wyoming. 1971.

Byrd, Forrest M. "Prolegomenon to Frederick Manfred." Doctoral Dissertation, University of Nebraska, 1975.

De Boer, Peter P. "Frederick Manfred: The Developing Art of the Novelist." Master's Thesis. The State University of Iowa, 1961.

Gits, Gordon P. "The Buckskin Man Tales of Frederick Manfred: Realistic or Naturalistic?" Master's Thesis, Mankato State College, 1971.

Hillnoe, Jean. "Themes of Isolation and Relationship in Selected Novels of Frederick Manfred." Master's Thesis, South Dakota State University, 1969.

Michael, Larry A. "Literary Allusions in the Fiction of Frederick Manfred." Master's Thesis, University of South Dakota, 1965.

Moen, Ole O. "The Voice of Siouxland: Man and Nature in Frederick Manfred's Writing." Doctoral Dissertation, University of Minnesota, 1978.

O'Brien, Richard P. "Naturalism and the Tragic View in the Writing of Frederick Manfred." Master's Thesis, Mankato State University, 1967.

Peet. Howard. "Evolution of a Man Named Fred." Master's Thesis. Moorhead State College, MN, 1965.

Pruett, Jacque. "A Critical Analysis of Lord Grizzly." Master's Thesis, Colorado State University, 1968.

Schultz, William E. "Frederick Manfred--The Siouxland Myth: A Study of the Myth's Purpose and its Influence on the Author." Master's Thesis, University of Wisconsin River Falls, 1968.

Sorenson, Charles Somner. "A Comparison of the Views of Hamsun, Rolvaag, and Feikema on Rural Society." Doctoral Dissertation, The State University of Iowa, 1965.

Spies III, George H. "John Steinbeck's The Grapes of Wrath and Frederick Manfred's The Golden Bowl: A Comparative Study." Doctoral Dissertation, Ball State University, 1973.

Ter Maat, Cornelius John. "Three Novelists and a Community: A Study of American Novelists with Dutch Calvinist Origins." Doctoral Dissertation, University of Michigan, 1963.

Section D: Book Reviews

One of the many ways to assess the impact of an author's work is through book reviews. They are usually written within the first few months of the release of a literary piece. While they do not have the lasting significance of critical essays or monographs, book reviews do, however, present a good picture of the immediate impact on the reading public. It is interesting to note with Manfred's works that both the number of reviews and geographical location of reviews differ greatly, depending on the particular book.

We compiled this list of reviews from the following sources: library searches, personal files, previous biliographies, Manfred's personal file, and the archives at the University of Minnesota. The last source is by far the most complete.

We did not include in our listing press releases or book reviews which were very short (one paragraph) and were in effect release announcements. There were at least two or three hundred of these.

Most reviews in Manfred's files and the University of Minnesota archives were clipped from newspapers or journals and included reviewer's name and date. Approximately sixty percent did not include page or section reference. Our procedure to locate these consisted primarily of the time-honored means of writing newspapers and journals, sometimes several times, and also many telephone calls. As one might expect, the small town newspapers were quick to respond, the big time papers recalcitrant or worse. Nonetheless, we managed to obtain definitive entries for all but forty reviews. We included the latter simply to evidence the scope of the reviews.

The review are ordered chronologically according to book as in Section A.

The Golden Bowl

Feld, Rose. New York Herald Tribune Weekly Book Review (October 1, 1944), p. 10.
Fridsma, Bernard. Frisian News Items, I (November, 1944), p. 3.
Isern, Thomas D. Chronicles of Oklahoma (Summer, 1977).
Johnson, Wendell. Chicago Sun Book Week (September 10, 1944), p. 3.
Parke, Andrea. New York Times (October 8, 1944), p. 14.

Preston, J.H. New Republic, CXI (October 30, 1944), p. 573.
Sherman, John K. Minneapolis Tribune (October 1, 1944).
Anonymous. The American Mercury, LX (March, 1945), p. 382.

Boy Almighty

A., D. Chicago Daily News (November 28, 1945), p. 19.
B., C. Washington Post (December 16, 1945), Sec. 5, p. 19.
Balakian, Nona. New York Times (January 13, 1946), p. 12.
Bontell, Chip. New York Post (November 28, 1945).
Cedor, Merwyn E. Chicago Daily Law Bulletin (January 16, 1946), p. 2.
Elwood, Irene. Los Angeles Times (December 2, 1945), Sec. III, p. 6.
Firebaugh, Joseph J. St. Louis Post-Dispatch (January 7, 1946), Sec. B, p. 2.
Fisher, Marcella N. Milwaukee Journal (December 9, 1945).
Gray, James. St. Paul Pioneer Press (December 2, 1945), Magazine Section, p. 4.
H., C. New York Sun (November 27, 1945).
H.,C.H. Your Health, XXXIII (November, 1951), p. 11.
Hardman, Henrietta. Hartford Courant Magazine (January 27, 1946).
Johnson, Wendell. Chicago Sun Book Week (December 9, 1945), p. 3.
Kranz, H.B. Saturday Review of Literature, XXVIII (December 22, 1945), p. 31.
Le Sueur, Meridel. The Worker (May 26, 1946).
MacDonald, Helen. Northwest Life, XVII (October, 1944), p. 19.
McDowell, Tremaine. Chicago Sunday Tribune (November 25, 1945), p. 11.
Miller, Anna. Chicago Bee (January 20, 1946), p. 16.
Olsen, Elizabeth W. Grand Rapids Herald (December 9, 1945), Sec. A, p. 12.
Rice, Jennings. New York Herald Tribune Weekly Book Review (December 9, 1945), p. 6.
Roberts, Mary Carter. Washington Star (December 23, 1945), Sec. B, p. 3.
Sherman, John K. Minneapolis Tribune (December 2, 1945), p. 19.
Smith, David. Sioux Falls Argus-Leader (November 11, 1945), p. 5.

Swan, Addie M. The Davenport [Iowa] Daily Times (December 29, 1945).
Anonymous. The American Mercury, LXII (February, 1946), p. 249.
Anonymous. De Volksvriend (November 29, 1945).
Anonymous. New Republic, CXIII (December 24, 1945), p. 877.
Anonymous. New Yorker, XXI (December 1, 1945), p. 128.
Anonymous. The Spectator (September 1, 1950), p. 264.

This Is The Year

Balakian, Nona. New York Times (March 30, 1947), p. 20.
Conroy, Jack. Philadelphia Enquirer (April 6, 1947).
Cournos, John. Philadelphia Bulletin (April 6, 1947), Book Review Section, p. 4.
Cross, Leslie. Milwaukee Journal (March 23, 1947).
Eikel, Fred. Dallas Times-Herald (April 27, 1947), Sec. 6, p. 7.
Farrelly, John. The New Republic, CXVI (April 14, 1947), p. 35.
Flanagan, J.T. Chicago Sun Book Week (March 23, 1947), p. 1.
Frederick, John T. Chicago Sun Book Week (May 4, 1947).
Fridsma, Bernard. The Calvin Forum, 12 (May, 1947), pp. 221-222.
Geisman, Maxwell. New York Herald Tribune (March 29, 1947), p. 12.
Gray, James. Chicago Daily News (April 1, 1947), p. 24.
Haas, Victor P. Omaha World-Herald (March 30, 1947), Sec. C, p. 24.
Havighurst, Walter. New York Herald Tribune Weekly Book Review (March 23, 1947), p. 10.
Healy, Ann. Hartford Courant (May 4, 1947).
J., E. San Francisco Chronicle (May 4, 1947), p. 13.
Jordan-Smith, Paul. Los Angeles Times (April 6, 1947).
L., E. A. Boston Globe (April 2, 1947), p. 19.
Lancaster, C. Maxwell. Nashville Barrier (April 16, 1947).
La Motte, Clyde. Houston Post (March 30, 1947).
North, Sterling. Washington Post (March 30, 1947), Sec. L, p. 7.
Rolfs, Alvin R. St. Louis Post Dispatch (May 1, 1947), Sec. B, p. 2.
Ross, J. L. Library Journal, LXXII (March 15, 1947), p. 462.
Schorer, Mark. Kenyon Review, IX (Autumn, 1947), pp. 628-636.

Sherman, John K. Minneapolis Tribune (March 30, 1947), p. 16.
Sikkema, Marten. Leervarder Courant [in Frisian] (February 10, 1965).
Smith, Harrison. Saturday Review Of Literature, XXX (March 29, 1947), p. 16.
Smith, Theodore. San Francisco Commercial News (April 19, 1947).
Snyder, Marjorie. Boston Herald (March 26, 1947), Sec. I, p. 3.
Sullivan, Julian T. Indianapolis Star (March 30, 1947), Sec. IV, p. 24.
Washburn, Beatrice. Miami Herald (May 4, 1947).
Watts, Dale K. Grand Rapids Herald (April 27, 1947), Sec. A, p. 10.
Anonymous. Kirkus Review, XV (January 15, 1947), p. 40.
Anonymous. New Yorker, XXIII (March 29, 1947), p. 106.
Anonymous. Time, XLIX (March 31, 1947), p. 105.

The Chokecherry Tree

Bateman, David. Cardiff [Wales, England] Western Mail (April 12, 1950).
Brown, E.S. Library Journal, LXXIII (April 15, 1948), p. 654.
Burger, Nash K. The New York Times Book Review (April 8, 1948), p. 23.
Conroy, Jack. Chicago Star (April 17, 1948).
Corey, Paul. New York Herald Tribune Weekly Book Review (August 22, 1948), p. 9.
Dedmon, Emmett. Chicago Sun Times (April 11, 1948).
Friedman, Robert. Daily Worker (May 11, 1948), p. 12.
Gault, Mark. Philadelphia Sunday Bulletin (April 11, 1948), p. 7.
Geismar, Maxwell. New York Herald Tribune (April 17, 1948).
Heilman, Robert B. Sewanee Review, LVI (Autumn 1948), pp. 671-679.
Hull, W.H. Mankato [Minn.] Free Press (June 25, 1948).
Jordan-Smith, Paul. Los Angeles Times (April 11, 1948), Sec. III, p. 4.
L., E. A. Boston Globe (April 14, 1948), p. 15.

La Motte, Clyde. Houston Post (April 18, 1948).
Mc Ghee, Willie M. Dallas Times Herald (May 9, 1948), Sec. 7, p. 5.
Miller, Nolan. The Antioch Review, VIII (Summer, 1948), p. 242.
O'Neil, Frank. Cleveland News (April 14, 1948).
Paulus, John D. Pittsburgh Press (April 25, 1948), p. 71.
Rogers, W. G. New York Post (April 9, 1948).
Sherman, John K. Minneapolis Tribune (April 11, 1948), Sec. W, p. 14.
Sherman, Thomas B. St. Louis Post Dispatch (April 12, 1948), Sec. B, p. 2.
Shulman, Max. Chicago Tribune (April 18, 1948).
Smith, David H. Sioux Falls Argus-Leader (April 18, 1948), p. 21.
Sullivan, Richard. New York Times Book Review (April 11, 1948), p. 7.
Symons, Julian. Manchester [England] Evening News (May 4, 1950).
Anonymous. Kirkus, XVI (March 1, 1948), p. 122.
Anonymous. New Yorker, XXIV (April 10, 1948), p. 121.

The Primitive

B., R. H. Durham [North Carolina] Morning Herald (September 18, 1949), Sec. D, p. 6.
B., V. A. Chicago News (September 14, 1949).
Bell, Blake Kennedy. Tulsa Daily World (September 18, 1949), Sec. 5, p. 9.
C., E. Columbus [Ohio] Dispatcher (September 25, 1949).
C., J. B. Newark News (October 16, 1949).
Chapin, Ruth. Christian Science Monitor (September 15, 1949), p. 15.
Corey, Paul. New York Herald Tribune Weekly Book Review (September 18, 1949), p. 9.
Dedmon, Emmett. Chicago Sun (September 18, 1949), Sec. X, p. 8.
Derleth, August. Chicago Sunday Tribune (September 18, 1949).
Ford, Jon. San Antonio Express (September 18, 1949), Sec. C, p. 8.
Friedman, Robert. Daily Worker (September 16, 1949), p. 13.

Gayne, Hazel. St. Paul Pioneer Press (September 14, 1949), Magazine Section, p. 12.

Gruenwald, Doris. Denver Post (October 16, 1949), Sec. C, p. 4.

Haas, Victor P. Omaha World Herald Magazine (September 25, 1949), Sec. C, p. 28.

Havighurst, Walter. Saturday Review of Literature (November 5, 1949).

Hughs, Riley. Commonweal, L (September 9, 1949), p. 538.

Jackson, Faith Reyher. Miami Herald (September 18, 1949), Sec. D, p. 4.

Jackson, Joseph Henry. San Francisco Chronicle (September 25, 1949), p. 20.

Jellema, Rod. Calvin College Chimes (September 22, 1949).

Jordan-Smith, Paul. Los Angeles Times (September 18, 1949), p. 9.

Laycock, E. A. Boston Globe (September 18, 1949), Sec. A, p. 41.

La Motte, Clyde. Houston Post (September 18, 1949).

Matthew, Christopher. The Milwaukee Journal (September 18, 1949), Sec. V, p. 4.

Munger, Stephen. Dallas News (September 18, 1949), Sec. VII, p. 11.

Nemerov, Howard. Sewanee Review, LVIII (Summer, 1950), pp. 539-540.

O'Bryant, Arch. Wichita Eagle (September 27, 1949), Sec. A, p. 6.

R., H. Kansas City Star (November 19, 1949).

R., W.G. Miami Sunday News Magazine (September 18, 1949), p. 19.

Reynolds, John. Cedar Rapids [Iowa] Gazette (September 18, 1949), Sec. 3, p. 2.

Rivette, Marc. San Francisco Chronicle (September 25, 1949), p. 20.

Rodgers, W. G. New York Post (Ocotober 8, 1949).

Scott, Virgil. Cleveland News (September 14, 1949).

Sherman, John K. Minneapolis Sunday Tribune (September 18, 1949), p. 15.

Smith, David H. Sioux Falls Argus-Leader (September 18, 1949), p. 13.

Snyder, Marjorie B. Boston Herald (September 21, 1949), p. 18.

Stewart, G. R. New York Times Book Review (September 18, 1949), p. 37.

Book Reviews 105

Truax, Charles. Dayton News (September 18, 1949), Sec. 3, p. 16.
W., B. C. Meriden [Conn.] Record (September 26, 1949), p. 6.
Warriner, Howard. Fort Wayne News Sentinel (November 26, 1949), p. 6.
Yanitelli, Victor. Best Sellers (September 15, 1949), p. 91.
Anonymous. Grand Rapids Press (August 19, 1949).
Anonymous. Kirkus, XVII (July 15, 1949), p. 370.
Anonymous. Minnesota Quarterly (Fall, 1949), pp. 35-37.
Anonymous. New Yorker, XXV (September 17, 1949), p. 106.
Anonymous. Time, LIV (September 19, 1949), p. 108.

The Brother

Borland, Hal. New York Times Book Review (December 17, 1950), p. 15.
Brennan, Dan. Minneapolis News (December 8, 1950).
Chapin, Ruth. Christian Science Monitor (November 7, 1950), p. 16.
Corey, Paul. New York Herald Tribune Book Review (November 26, 1950), p. 16.
Dedman, Emmett. Chicago Sun Times (October 24, 1950), p. 6.
Haas, Victor P. Omaha World Herald Magazine (December 3, 1950), Sec. C, p. 28.
Jellema, Rod. Calvin College Chimes (December 8, 1950), p. 4.
Jordan-Smith, Paul. Los Angeles Times (November 5, 1950), Sec. IV, p. 7.
L., E. A. Boston Globe (November 5, 1950), Sec. A. p. 25.
M., J. L. Durham [North Carolina] Herald (November 12, 1950), Sec. D, p. 6.
Matthew, Christopher. The Milwaukee Sunday Journal (October 29, 1950), Sec. V, p. 4.
O'Bryant, Arch. Wichita Eagle (November 26, 1950), Sec. A, p. 6.
Patnode, Jack. St. Paul Pioneer Press (October 29, 1950), p. 12.
Reynolds, John. Cedar Rapids [Iowa] Gazette (November 5, 1950), Sec. 2, p. 8.
Rogers, W. C. New Haven Register (November 12, 1950).
Rothermel, J.F. Birmingham Sunday News (November 5, 1950), Sec. C, p. 12.

Schott, Webster. St. Louis Post Dispatch (December 11, 1950), Sec. B, p. 2.
Sherman, John K. Minneapolis Tribune (October 29, 1950), Sec. F, p. 10.
Slain, Bob. Charlotte [North Carolina] News (November 4, 1950).
Smith, David H. Sioux Falls Argus-Leader (October 29, 1950). p. 22.
Strong, Russell A. Kalamazoo Gazette (December 13, 1950), p. 10.
Sullivan, Richard. Chicago Sunday Tribune (November 12, 1950), p. 25.
Tozer, Eliot. Boston Herald (November 5, 1950), Sec. B, p. 8.
W., B. J. Columbia Missourian (February 8, 1951), p. 4.
Walsch, Anne. Dallas Daily Times (December 31, 1950), Sec. 5, p. 6.
Anonymous. Kirkus, XVIII (September 1, 1950), p. 529.
Anonymous. New Yorker, XXVI (November 18, 1950), p. 185.

The Giant

Barkam, John. Dallas Times Herald (December 30, 1951), Sec. 3, p. 5.
Beeler, A. J. Louisville Courier-Journal (January 27, 1952), Sec. 3, p. 12.
Brantley, Russell. Durham [North Carolina] Herald (January 20, 1952), Sec. D, p. 6.
Butcher, Fanny. Chicago Sunday Tribune (December 30, 1951), p. 5.
Cody, Ernest. Columbus Dispatch (January 6, 1952), Sec. F, p. 7.
Corey, Paul. New York Herald Tribune Book Review (December 30, 1951), p. 8.
D., W. Houston Post (December 30, 1951).
Dedman, Emmett. Chicago Sun Times (December 30, 1951).
Etzhorn, L. R. Library Journal, LXXVI (December 15, 1951), p. 2111.
Gayne, Hazel. St. Paul Pioneer Press (January 6, 1952), p. 16.
Haas, Victor P. Omaha World Herald (January 27, 1952), Sec. G, p. 25.
Hicks, Granville. New York Times Book Review (December 30, 1951), p. 5.
Hughs, Riley. Catholic World, CLXXIV (March, 1952), p. 470.
Jones, Carter Brooks. Washington Star (December 30, 1951), Sec. C, p. 3.

Jordan-Smith, Paul. Los Angeles Times (December 30, 1951), Sec. 3, p. 12.
Laycock, Edward A. Boston Globe (December 30, 1951), Sec. A, p. 7.
Little, Carl Victor. San Francisco News (January 11, 1952).
Lovell, Florence. Bridgeport [Conn.] Post (January 9, 1952), Sec. B, p. 4.
Matthew, Christopher. Milwaukee Journal (December 30, 1952).
North, Sterling. Washington Post (December 30, 1951), Sec. B, p. 6.
Parsons, Margaret. Worcester Telegram (December 30, 1951), Sec. D, p. 7.
Rothermel, J. F. Birmingham News (December 30, 1951), Sec. F, p. 6.
Sadler, H. Ft. Wayne New-Sentinel (January 12, 1952), p. 4.
Salemson, Harold J. New York Compass (February 4, 1952), p. 9.
Schott, Webster. Kansas City Star (January 26, 1952).
Seward, William W. Norfolk Virginian Pilot (December 30, 1951).
Sherman, John K. Minneapolis Tribune (December 30, 1951), Sec. G, p. 12.
Smith, Harrison. Saturday Review, XXXV (January 12, 1952), p. 14.
Snyder, Marjorie. Boston Herald (January 6, 1952), Sec. I, p. 3.
Truax, Charles. Dayton News (December 30, 1951), Sec. 2, p. 2.
Anonymous. Kirkus Review, XIX (November 1, 1951), p. 640.
Anonymous. New Yorker, XXVII (December 29, 1951), p. 65.
Anonymous. San Francisco Chronicle (March 16, 1952), p. 18.

Lord Grizzly

Adams, J. Donald. New York Times Book Review (October 31, 1954), p. 40.
Baker, Marcia. Cincinnati Enquirer (October 17, 1954), p. 48.
Becket, Roger. Long Island Sunday Press (October 10, 1954), p. 40.
Edgerton, Jay. The Minnesota Star (September 26, 1954).
Flanagan, John. Minnesota History. (Spring 1955), pp. 210-211.
Haas, Victor P. New York Times (September 26, 1954), p. 32.
Havighurst, Walter. New York Herald Tribune Book Review (November 28, 1954), p. 14.
Jacks, L. V. Books on Trial (November 1954), p. 73.

Jones, Madison. New York Times Book Review (February 16, 1975), p. 6.
Leonard, J. The Daily Plainsman (October 10, 1954), p. 2.
Markson, Robert J. Sacramento Bee (February 10, 1955), Sec. F, p. 14.
Matthew, Christopher. Milwaukee Journal (November 21, 1954).
Sherman, John K. Minneapolis Sunday Tribune (September 26, 1954), p. 14.
Sullivan, Richard. Chicago Sunday Tribune (October 3, 1954), p. 3.
W., R. L. Providence Journal (October 17, 1954).
Williams, John. The Nation, CXCIII (November 18, 1961), pp. 401-406.
Anonymous. Bookmark [New York State Library], XIV (November 1954), p. 35.
Anonymous. Booklist, LI (December 15, 1954), p. 176.
Anonymous. Indianapolis News (November 2, 1954), p. 2.
Anonymous. Kirkus Review, XXII (July 15, 1954), p. 451.
Anonymous. Los Angeles Times (November 14, 1954), Sec. IV, p. 7.
Anonymous. Springfield Republican (October 17, 1954), Sec. C, p. 9.

Morning Red

Brewer, Barbara. Virginian-Pilot (December 23, 1956), Sec. B, p. 8.
Conroy, Jack. The American Book Collector, VIII (March, 1957), p. 20.
Fisher, Vardis. Gooding [Idaho] Leader (March 14, 1957), Sec. II, p. 2.
Fuller, Edmund. Chicago Sunday Tribune (January 20, 1957), p. 8.
Haas, Victor P. New York Times Book Review (February 17, 1957), p. 28.
Johnson, Robert J.R. St. Paul Pioneer Press (January 6, 1957), p. 11.
K. L. Denver Post (December 9, 1956), p. 12.
Kreiger, Robert E. Worchester [Mass.] Telegram (December 2, 1956), Sec. E, p. 7.
Milton, John R. The Cresset, XX (September, 1957), pp. 27-28.
Sherman, John K. Minneapolis Sunday Tribune (December 2, 1956), Sec. E, p. 6.

Schiller, Andrew. Chicago Sun Times (December 30, 1956), Sec. 3, p. 4.
Shore, Janet. Ivory Tower [University of Minnesota] (December 10, 1956), p. 15.
Anonymous. Saturday Review, XI (January 26, 1957), p. 32.

Riders of Judgment

Adams, Joe. Indianapolis News (July 27, 1957), p. 2.
Ball, Keith. Miami News (June 28, 1957).
Billings, Jim. Springfield [Mo.] News and Leader (May 26, 1957), Sec. B, p. 5.
Conroy, Jack. Chicago Sun Times (June 2, 1957), Sec. 3, p. 6.
Carver, Wayne. St. Louis Dispatch (July 5, 1957), Sec. B, p. 2.
G., F. J. Columbia Missourian (June 13, 1957), p. 4.
Gould, Alphin T. Providence Sun Journal (May 6, 1957).
Haas, Victor P. Chicago Sunday Tribune (May 26, 1957). p. 5.
Havighurst, Walter. New York Herald Tribune Book Review (July 28, 1957), p. 7.
Idzal, Milton M. Sioux City Journal (June 16, 1957), Sec. 3, p. 4.
Jones, Madison. New York Times Book Review (February 16, 1957), p. 6.
L., E. A. Boston Globe (June 16, 1957), Sec. A, p. 27.
Mansten, S. P. Saturday Review, XL (June 1, 1957), p. 31.
Milton, John R. The Cresset, XXI (May, 1958), p. 27.
Nibbelink, Herman. Calvin College Chimes (February 20, 1957), p. 5.
Nordyke, Lewis. New York Times (May 26, 1957). p. 2.
O'Leary, Jerry O. Washington Star (June 23, 1957), Sec. E, p. 7.
Sherman, John K. Minneapolis Tribune (May 26, 1957), p. 14.
Smith, David H. Sioux Falls Argus-Leader (May 26, 1957), Sec. C, p. 9.
Swallow, Alan. Denver Sunday Post (May 19, 1957), p. 10.
Anonymous. Kirkus Review, XXV (March 15, 1957), p. 233.

Conquering Horse

Ball, Keith. Miami News (June 28, 1959).

Blacker, I. R. Saturday Review, XLII (July 25, 1959), p. 23.
Carver, Wayne. St. Louis Dispatch (July 5, 1959), Sec. D, p. 4.
Cleary, John. Hartford Times (July 3, 1959).
Conroy, Jack. Chicago Sun Times (August 2, 1959).
Eddy, Bob. St. Paul Dispatch (June 27, 1959). p. 4.
Engle, Paul. Chicago Sunday Tribune (June 28, 1959), p. 3.
Engle, Paul. New York Times Book Review (June 28, 1959), p. 4.
Fisher, Vardis. Gooding [Idaho] Leader (September 10, 1959), Sec. II, p. 2.
Havighurst, Walter. New York Herald Tribune Book Review (July 5, 1959), p. 5.
Huseboe, Arthur R. Report [University of South Dakota], IX (Spring, 1961), pp. 20-24.
Hutchinson, W. H. San Francisco Chronicle (August 2, 1959), p. 16.
Jones, Madison. New York Times Book Review (February 16, 1975), p. 6.
Kennedy, Wm. G. Bridgeport [Conn.] Post (July 19, 1959), Sec. B, p. 41.
Schmuck, John. Library Journal, LXXXIV (August 1959), p. 2375.
Sherman, John K. Minneapolis Tribune (June 28, 1959), p. 6.
Smith, David. Sioux Falls Argus-Leader (June 21, 1959), Sec. C, p. 17.
Walt, James. Washington Post (June 28, 1959).
Anonymous. Kirkus Review, XXVII (May 1, 1959), p. 327.
Anonymous. Wilson Library Bulletin, LV (September, 1959), p. 447.

Arrow Of Love

Aardema, Harold. The Doon [Iowa] Reminder (September 7, 1961), p. 1.
Chernoff, Melva G. Sioux Falls Argus-Leader (September 17, 1961), Sec. B, p. 7.
Eddy, Bob. St. Paul Dispatch (September 9, 1961), p. 4.
Egan, Ferol. San Francisco Examiner (January 7, 1962).
Levin, Martin. New York Times (October 15, 1961), p. 48.
Reedy, Mary E. Omaha World-Herald (September 23, 1962), Sec. G, p. 25.

Sherman, John K. Minneapolis Sunday Tribune (November 26, 1961), p. 6.
VanderMeer, Virginia. Calvin College Chimes, LVI (March 2, 1962), p. 2.

Wanderlust

Benson, Earl. St. Paul Dispatch (March 30, 1963), p. 3.
C., M. G. Sioux Falls Argus-Leader (February 3, 1963), Sec. C, p. 9.
Klement, Dave. The Sunday Oklahoman (January 27, 1963), Sec. D, p. 3.
Matthew, Christopher. Chicago Daily News (January 23, 1963), p. 26.
Milton, John R. Minneapolis Sunday Tribune (May 5, 1963), Editorial Section, p. 6.
Smith, David H. Sioux Falls Argus-Leader (February 3, 1963), p. 9.

Winter Count

S., D. H. Sioux Falls Argus-Leader (November 6, 1966), Sec. C, p. 17.
Smith, Ray. Minneapolis Tribune (November 20, 1966), Sec. E, p. 2.
Anonymous. Library Journal, XCII (February 15, 1967), p. 781.

Scarlet Plume

C., P. M. St. Paul Pioneer Press (November 15, 1964), Lively Arts Section, p. 17.
Haas, Victor P. Omaha Sunday World-Herald (December 6, 1964), Sec. F, p. 9.
Haas, Joseph and Bradley Van Allen. Chicago Daily News Panorama (November 28, 1964), p. 5.
Havens, Lori. The Columbian Missourian (January 16, 1966), p. 11.
Jones, Madison. New York Times Book Review (February 16, 1975) p. 6.
Markson, Robert. Sacramento Bee (December 13, 1964), Sec. L, p. 23.

Matthew, Christopher. Milwaukee Journal (February 7, 1965).
McIntosh, Al. Luverne [Minn.] Rock County Star-Herald (November 26, 1964), pp. 1, 4.
Metlova, Maria. Van Nuys News (April 2, 1965), Sec. A, p. 34.
Miller, William G. Boston Globe (January 12, 1965), p. 27.
Sherman, John K. Minneapolis Tribune (November 22, 1964), Sec. E, p. 6.
Smith, David Hubbard. Sioux Falls Argus-Leader (December 20, 1964), Sec. C, p. 11.
Sprague, Marshall. New York Times Book Review (November 22, 1964), p. 50.
Suggs, Martha. Columbus [Ga.] Enquirer (January 11, 1965), p. 8.
Wentz, Roby. Los Angeles Times (December 20, 1964), Calendar Section, p. 18.
Anonymous. Sioux City Journal (December 20, 1964), Sec. C, p. 4.

The Man Who Looked Like The Prince Of Wales

A., L. D. The Fresno Bee (November 7, 1965), Sec. F, p. 19.
Bert, Norman A. South Bend Tribune (October 10, 1965), p. 12.
Boardman, Kathryn. St. Paul Pioneer Press (September 12, 1965), p. 17.
Engle, Paul. Chicago Daily News Panorama (September 25, 1965), p. 7.
Fowler, Helen V. Los Angeles Times (January 23, 1966), Calender Section, p. 26.
Goodyear, Lucille J. Arizona Republic (November 7, 1965).
Haas, Victor P. Omaha World-Herald (October 3, 1965), Sec. I, p. 29.
Leven, Martin. New York Times Book Review (November 14, 1965), p. 63.
Matthew, Christopher. Milwaukee Journal (November 7, 1965).
Milton, John R. Saturday Review (November 6, 1965), p. 69.
S., D. H. Sioux Falls Argus-Leader (September 26, 1965), Sec. C, p. 13.
Sherman, John K. Minneapolis Tribune (September 26, 1965), Sec. X, p. 10.
Anonymous. Best Sellers, XXV (October 1, 1965), p. 271.
Anonymous. Sioux City Journal (November 21, 1965), Sec. C, p. 8.

King Of Spades

Barkham, John. Philadelphia Sunday Bulletin (September 4, 1966), p. 3.
C., P. M. St. Paul Pioneer Press (October 23, 1966), p. 27.
Conroy, Jack. Chicago Daily News (October 29, 1966), Panorama Section, p. 10.
Delahan, William. Pittsburgh Press (November 20, 1966), Sec. 6, p. 6.
Derleth, August. Madison Capital Times (November 24, 1966), Sec. P, p. 34.
Fowler, Helen V. Los Angeles Times (October 9, 1966), p. 26.
Garfield, Brian. Saturday Review, XLIX (October 22, 1966). p. 57.
Gosnell, John S. Norfolk Virginian Pilot (January 22, 1967).
Haas, Victor P. Chicago Tribune (November 20, 1966), p. 11.
Hanna, Pat. Rocky Mountain News (December 4, 1966), Sec. A, p. 23.
Jones, Madison. New York Times Book Review (February 16, 1975), p. 6.
Kriessling, E. C. Milwaukee Journal (December 25, 1966).
Lopez, Eddie. Fresno Bee (December 18, 1966), Sec. F, p. 16.
McCabe, Adeline. Casper Wyoming Star Tribune (November 26, 1966).
Miller, Doris B. Roanoke Times (November 13, 1966), Sec. C, p. 8.
Read, David W. St. Louis Post Dispatch (March 12, 1967), Sec. C, p. 4.
Roth, Russell. Western American Literature, I (Winter, 1967). pp. 302-304.
S., D. H. Sioux Falls Argus-Leader (November 6, 1966), Sec. C, p. 17.
Sherman, John K. Minneapolis Tribune (October 23, 1966), Sec. E, p. 6.
Tierney, Joseph B. South Bend Tribune (December 25, 1966), p. 8.
Anonymous. Best Sellers, XXVI (December 1, 1966), p. 323.
Anonymous. Kirkus Review, XXXIV (August 1, 1966), p. 788.
Anonymous. Library Journal, XCI (October 15, 1966), p. 4974.
Anonymous. New York Times Book Review (December 18, 1966), p. 20.
Anonymous. Publishers Weekly (June 20, 1966), p. 66.
Anonymous. Publishers Weekly (February 4, 1974), p. 101.
Anonymous. Sioux City Journal (October 23, 1966), Sec. B, p. 11.
Anonymous. Virginia Kirkus Service (October 9, 1966).

Apples Of Paradise

Donaldson, Scott. Minneapolis Tribune (May 5, 1968), Sec. E, p. 7.
Fiedler, Patricia. Quincy [Mass.] Patriot Ledger (July 2, 1968) p. 24.
Gassiott, Vicky. Tulsa World (May 6, 1968), Sec. E, p. 18.
Goodyear, Lucille J. Arizona Republic (June 14, 1968).
Haas, Joseph. Toledo [Ohio] Blade (June 23, 1968), Sec. G, p. 5.
Rose, Jeanne. Baltimore Evening Sun (May 19, 1968), Sec. D, p. 4.
S., D. H. Sioux Falls Argus-Leader (March 24, 1968), Sec. C, p. 15.
Simpson, Elizabeth. Fresno Bee (May 19, 1968), Sec. F, p. 27.
Westbrook, Max. Western American Literature, II (Summer 1968), pp. 157-158.
Anonymous. Choice, V (October, 1968), p. 954
Anonymous. Honolulu Star Bulletin (April 28, 1968), Aloha Magazine, p. 25.
Anonymous. Kirkus Review, XXXVI (January 1, 1968), p. 24.
Anonymous. Library Journal, XCIII (March 15, 1968), p. 1162.
Anonymous. Publishers Weekly, CXCIII (January 22, 1968), p. 269.

Eden Prairie

Bautista, Pat. Long Beach Independent (November 21, 1968), Sec. A, p. 2.
Conroy, Jack. Chicago News (October 5, 1968).
Donaldson, Scott. Minneapolis Tribune (December 1, 1968), Sec. E, p. 17.
Hackett, Polly. Fort Wayne New-Sentinel (October 5, 1968), Sec. A, p. 4.
Hughes, Catherine. Chicago Sun Times (October 13, 1968).
McDermott, Mary S. St. Louis Globe Democrat (October 5, 1968), Sec. G, p. 5.
Meyer, Gerald. Des Moines Register (December 8, 1968), Sec. T, p. 13.
Neil, Leonard. Worthington [Minn] Globe (October 3, 1968), p. 3.
Newton Jr., Virgil M. Tampa Tribune (February 2, 1969), Sec. C, p. 5.

Book Reviews 115

Read, David W. St. Louis Post Dispatch (October 20, 1968), Sec. C, p. 4.
Rose, Jeanne. Baltimore Sunday Sun (October 13, 1968), Sec. D, p. 5.
S., D. H. Sioux Falls Argus-Leader (September 29, 1968), Sec. C, p. 14.
Schroeder, William H. Best Sellers (October 15, 1968), p. 290.
Schuster, Marjorie. Cleveland Press (November 8, 1968), p. 19.
Sherman, John K. Minneapolis Star (September 27, 1968), Sec. A, p. 15.
Westbrook, Max. Western American Literature, III (Winter 1969), pp. 307-309.
Anonymous. Kirkus Review, XXXVI (July 1, 1968), p. 716.
Anonymous. Publishers Weekly, CXCIV (July 15, 1968), p. 54.
Anonymous. Sioux City Journal (November 17, 1968), Sec. D, p. 10.

Conversations With Manfred

Aardema, Harold. The Doon [Iowa] Press (August 29, 1974), p. 1.
Anderson, David D. Society For The Study Of Midwestern Literature News Letter, V (Spring, 1975).
Bjerk, Irid. Luverne [Minn.] Star-Herald (August 28, 1974), Sec. B, p. 2.
Etulian, Richard W. American West (January, 1975), p. 54.
Faber, Paul. Calvin College Chimes (February 14, 1975), p. 7.
Flanagan, John T. Minnesota History (Spring, 1976), pp. 36-37.
Griffith, Roger. Chicago Sun-Times (March 2, 1975), Sec. B, p. 8.
Grumback, Doris. The New Republic (September 14, 1974), p. 32.
Roth, Russell. Minneapolis Tribune (December 15, 1974), Sec. D, p. 12.
Spies, George H. Western American Literature, X (Spring, 1975), pp. 77-78.
Timmerman, John J. The Reformed Journal (October, 1974), pp. 22-23.
Anonymous. Booklist, LXXII (December 15, 1975), p. 564.
Anonymous. The Literary Tabloid, I (February, 1975), p. 22.
Anonymous. Reprint Bulletin - Book Review, XXIII (1978), p. 33.
Anonymous. Sioux Falls Argus-Leader (September 1, 1974), Sec. B, p. 2.

The Manly-Hearted Woman

Anderson, David. Society For The Study of Midwestern Literature Newsletter, VI (Spring, 1976), p. 1.
Bjerk, Irid. Luverne [Minn.] Star-Herald (March 24, 1976), p. 11.
Cheuse, Alan. Los Angeles Times (June 27, 1976), Calendar Section, p. 11.
Frakes, James R. New York Times Book Review (May 23, 1976), p. 38.
Griffith, Roger. Chicago Sun Times (February 29, 1976), Sec. III, p. 7.
Griffith, R. P. Kankakee Star-News (May 13, 1976).
Gruchow, Paul. Worthington [Minn.] Globe (July 6, 1976), p. 3.
Grumback, Doris. Washington Post (March 23, 1976), Sec. B, p. 6.
Laine, William. Minneapolis Tribune (February 15, 1976), Sec. D, p. 11.
Thornton, Eugenia. Cleveland Plain Dealer (March 21, 1976), Sec. V, p. 9.
Timmerman, John J. Reformed Journal (May-June, 1976), pp. 36-37.
Anonymous. America, CXXXV (November 13, 1976), p. 332.
Anonymous. Booklist, LXXII (January 15, 1976), p. 667.
Anonymous. Kirkus Review, XLIII (October 15, 1975), p. 1207.
Anonymous. Library Journal, CI (February 15, 1976), p. 636.
Anonymous. Publishers Weekly (March 2, 1976).
Anonymous. St. Paul Pioneer Press (December 28, 1975), p. 6.
Anonymous. Sioux Falls Argus-Leader (April 4, 1976), Sec. C, p. 18.

Milk Of Wolves

Aardema, Harold. The Doon [Iowa] Press (April 15, 1976), p. 1.
Griffith, R. P. Kankakee Star-News (May 13, 1976).
S., P. C. Lyon County [Iowa] Reporter (May 12, 1976), p. 4.
Spavin, Don. St. Paul Pioneer Press (May 9, 1976), p. 7.
Wright, Robert C. Minneapolis Tribune (July 11, 1976), Sec. D, p. 10.
Westbrook, Max. Western American Literature, XI (Winter, 1977), pp. 353-354.
Anonymous. Booklist, LXXIII (December 15, 1976), p. 588.

Green Earth

Brunt, Bayard. Philadelphia Sunday Bulletin (May 14, 1978), Focus Section, p. 8.
Cheuse, Alan. Los Angeles Times Book Review (January 1, 1978), p. 4.
DeMers, John. Houston Chronicle (January 22, 1978), Zest Magazine Section, p. 14.
Flora, Joseph M. Midwestern Miscellany: The Society For The Study of Midwestern Literature, VII (1979), pp. 56-63.
Glewive, June E. Sioux Falls Argus-Leader (December 11, 1977), Sec. C, p. 1.
Huyser, Joan. Calvin College Chimes (January 26, 1979), p. 7.
Jones, Waring. Western American Literature, XIV (May, 1979), pp. 69-70.
Larson, Charles R. Chicago Tribune (November 20, 1977).
McAllister, Nick. Denver Sunday Post (March 19, 1978), p. 67.
McKown, Deborah. Houston Post (November 20, 1977).
Mason, Anne. Milwaukee Journal (March 12, 1978), Sec. 5, p. 3.
Remele, Larry. South Dakota History, VIII (Summer, 1978), pp. 271-272.
Roth, Russell. Des Moines Sunday Register (January 1, 1978), Sec. B, p. 5.
Roth, Russell. Minneapolis Tribune (November 27, 1977), Sec. D, p. 16.
Sandburg, Helga. New York Times Book Review (January 22, 1978), pp. 15, 21.
Schaap, James. Doon [Iowa] Press (November 3, 1977), p. 4.
Schaap, James. Sioux Center [Iowa] News (November 2, 1977), p. 10.
Timmerman, John H. Grand Rapids Press (February 19, 1978), Sec. F, p. 2.

Anonymous. Booklist, LXXIV (November 1, 1977), p. 463.
Anonymous. Bookviews (October, 1977), p. 22.
Anonymous. Kirkus Review, XLV (September 1, 1977), p. 950.
Anonymous. Library Journal, CII (January 22, 1978), p. 15.
Anonymous. Luverne [Minn.] Star-Herald (November 16, 1977), p. 5.
Anonymous. Publishers Weekly (October 10, 1977), p. 74.

The Wind Blows Free

Aardema, Harold. Doon [Iowa] Press (August 2, 1979), p. 2.
Bjerk, Irid. Luverne [Minn.] Star Herald (September 12, 1979), Sec. B, p. 3.
Flora, Joseph M. Newsletter of the Society for the Study of Midwestern Literature, IX (Fall 1979), pp. 6, 7.
Hudson, Lew. Worthington [Minn] Globe (August 17, 1979).
Koerselman, Glada. Le Mars [Iowa] Daily Sentinel (September 20, 1979), p. 1.
Milton, John R. Minneapolis Tribune (October 7, 1979).
S., P. C. Lyon County [Iowa] Reporter (September 5, 1979), p. 3.
Timmerman, John J. The Reformed Journal, XXX (March, 1980).

Narrative Interview

Certainly one of the most troublesome aspects about being an author is getting published. Finding and keeping a publisher can be an arduous task. The interview which follows is Manfred's recollection of the difficulty, and sometimes ease, which he experienced in getting his works published.

Manfred is a superb storyteller with an extraordinary memory. Interspersed in the publishing history are a multitude of interesting autobiographical tidbits which tell us about the man and the author.

The interview took place in late August, 1979. The setting was his small "writing cabin" located about one hundred feet from his home. He does most of his writing there during the morning hours. Inside are two chairs, a desk, the old Remington 17 typewriter he has used for all of his works, files, and a small library of some of his favorite writers. On the west wall above the window are copies of all his works, in the order they were published, both hardcover and paperback. The interviewer, Rod Mulder, began the interview by pointing to The Golden Bowl and asking about the history of its publication. At various times during the two-hour taped interview, Manfred or Mulder would make reference to books that were situated on the shelf.

The Golden Bowl went through at least seven drafts. The early drafts I called Of These It Is Said. The University of Minnesota archives have all the different drafts and also some of the rejection slips which I kept.

One of the drafts went to Modern Age Books. They had kind of a liberal, left-wing publishing there for a while. They liked the third draft I sent them, but they asked me to rewrite it and put in a revolutionary or proletariat ending. Well, I of course couldn't do that. I'd heard enough preaching in my life in the Christian Reformed Church, without wanting to put in a little preaching about the left-wing business, all of which I didn't exactly agree with anyway. I had a liberal bent of mind, but I wasn't that liberal or left-wing.

There were some other rejections that were of interest. Norton looked at it and said they liked it a lot, but that I should rewrite it and work on it some more and some day they'd like to see it again. A man named Latham there was very kind to me. I talked to him one day. He had many nice little things to tell me. For example, he told me to be sure to use that space bar more. I had a way of not putting enough space between sentences; they looked like they were run in.

Then, about the sixth draft, I was told there was a man in St. Paul working for the Webb publishing company by the name of Paul C. Hillestad. Later on I dedicated The Chokecherry Tree to him. I called him up and asked him if it was true that he was going to publish fiction. Up to that point, they had published farm manuals and farm text books, and were very successful at it, but they wanted to go into what they called trade publishing which would include fiction. Hillestad said, "Yes." So I said, "Well, I got a bunch of manuscripts." And Hillestad said, "Who told you about me?" And I said, "Helen Clapesattle." She was then at the University of Minnesota Press and was the author of Doctors Mayo. That was once a great bestseller. "Well," he says, "that's fine. Helen comes highly recommended, so why don't you come over." And he set a date. I brought him . . . he told me to bring him all the versions of The Golden Bowl, two versions of This Is The Year, and one version of a book that I have just now finished, called Sons of Adam. This I think was somewhere in the fall or late summer of '43. I didn't hear from him for a long, long time. One day the phone rang and he says, "I'd like to talk to you about the manuscripts you brought over." I went to meet him at his office. I rode the Oak Harriet streetcar from Minneapolis to St. Paul. He took me out to lunch at the Covered Wagon. I'll never forget that. It was the first time I ever tasted Old Forester bourbon -- a kind of smoky bourbon. We each had a highball along with Lake Superior trout.

We went back to his office and talked some more. He had these manuscripts in front of him. He first took hold of what later on became Sons of Adam, which at that time I called A Time To Remember. He went through those 800 pages and talked about them a little bit, and then said, "This is not ready for publication." He set them off to the side. Then he took hold of the two versions of This Is the Year and commented about them, said that I had got hold of a very good idea there, but it looked too much like I was safety-pinning various things together. I would take a little item of a previous chapter and make that the beginning of the next, and he felt that it looked like a bunch of safety pins holding together a bunch of diapers. Which is a good description. He said there were some stories in it worth salvaging. And I did salvage some stories out of there which later on showed up in Apples of Paradise. Then he set those aside. Then he picked up The Golden Bowl. At that time I called it The Golden Bowl is Broken. He went through the first draft and made comments on that, then the second, then the third. Two of the versions were in play form. The Federal Theatre project in Minneapolis and St. Paul was going to put in on at one time. I had acts written and was working on the third. The kids in the acting group were really working on it, memorizing it and rehearsing it. I'd sit there listening to them and if the dialogue didn't fit their mouths right, I'd rewrite it for them as it went along. At night I'd add a new part. We were that far along when Senator Millard Tydings of Maryland decided that that government thing should be cancelled and he passed a resolution to drop the Federal Theatre project. That was the end of that idea for a play. Who knows, I might have been a playwriter had that gone through.

Hillestad went on down to the last version, the sixth. By the time he got to the sixth, I thought, he's going to turn everything down. When he finished with the sixth he said, "You know, this is very good. This is publishable. But I'd like to have you go home and do it one more time. Rewrite the whole thing and then bring it back." So I packed all the stuff up, all the manuscripts. There was a considerable pile there. I went home and at that point I really got excited. Here was, at last, a chance to get printed. This is after Knopf, Scribners, Macmillan, Random House, a whole host of them, had turned down everything I had ever sent off, including The Golden Bowl. There were I believe two rejections by Knopf. I did start rewriting it pretty thoroughly and I dropped some things and put in some other things and gradually it began to take shape. The last third or so, I added a whole bunch of new things which were never in the other drafts. That's why the first half of the book is sort of jerky and scattered. There are also still some remnants left of stage instructions in the first chapter. Which goes back to that stage version. But about where Maury goes into The Badlands, from there on, that was all new. That takes off as a kind of separate narration. When you read the book, you'll notice that it kind of speeds up there and goes pretty good.

So I brought the seventh version to Hillestad and he called later to say that he liked it very much and he'd like to make out a contract for it. He had only one reservation which was that the opening paragraph of each chapter was too thick. I had worked on a newspaper for two years and learned to put everything in the first paragraph. I went back and knocked them all out and rewrote them, simplified them, and just had a couple simple sentences to start out. That was about all we did to it. And he made one additional cut when I was gone that I never liked and I had that restored in the second printing.

It's an interesting story how we signed a contract. When we were done editing and there was nothing more to do, I'd visit him once in awhile and say, "Well, how's it getting along?" He always turned a little red and he didn't know what to say. Finally the following happened. I was sitting there talking to him across his desk and I noticed he had three baskets on his desk. One was marked "In," one "Out," and the other "Miscellaneous." In Miscellaneous I was several blue legal documents or papers folded as legal documents usually are. Now, I had seen contracts that he'd shown me which he had given to other authors, so it hit me, as I was talking to him, "That's got to be my contract."

When there was kind of a pause in the dialogue, I reached over and I picked them up and opened one up, and sure enough, the contract was for me. I leaned back and said, "Tell you what, Paul. I only have my wife behind me, who has a little job at the University of Minnesota-- something like 50 bucks or so a month-- and then I earn a little bit once in a while working for a little newspaper. And you got the millions of Webb publishing behind you. Look, I'm willing to take a gamble with you." So I started signing it.

"Hey, just a minute," he said. He was real red-faced. "Aurelia. Come in here a minute." Aurelia Smith was his secretary. She came in and she witnessed the signing. And that's how my first book got printed. Now, I literally had to pull that contract . . . . like pulling teeth, you know. Then I found out the reason he was hesitant was that the linotypists in the plant had objected to the sexy scenes in the book. They told the two owners they were going to quit. They had only done farm manuals before that! Yeh, but you see, no breeding, no breeding in my book. Ha. One of the partners was fine but the other was not.

Then we proceeded on to <u>Boy Almighty</u>. There wasn't any problem there. Hillestad liked that book. He objected to some of the strong stuff in it. And there was . . . I guess there was some more argument from the guys down in the linotype room, but by that time they had cooled off some. <u>This Is the Year</u> he liked and he wanted to do it. But, old Harmon, one of the partners at Webb, died. And then Reuel Harmon, his son, who had just returned from the war and didn't really know what was going on, wasn't too hot about going on with the fiction. Particularly since old Klein, the other owner, said they'd have to stop all fiction.

Paul Hillestad wanted to hang on to This Is the Year. Paul was kind of thinking about going to Knopf and thought that Knopf might bring it out. When The Golden Bowl came out with good reviews in the "The New Leader," "The New York Times," and "The New York Sun," and one other New York paper, old Knopf instantly wired me and then tried to telephone me to get my contract. In response, I sent him a copy of the rejections they had sent me earlier. But Knopf persisted and tried to get Paul Hillestad to leave Webb and become one of his editors so he could have me. But Paul's wife didn't want to move to New York. Actually Paul himself wasn't too hot about it either. He wanted to set up a Western House. So that fell through.

One day when I was visiting Sinclair Lewis up in Duluth, he suggested that I had to get away from Webb, go to "New York where they really push things. They know how to merchandise fiction." Hillestad had already made some arrangement with the Curtis Brown Ltd. literary agency to sell my books for Webb abroad and to the movies. So I was in a sense already halfway in with the Curtis Brown agency. Lewis was with Curtis Brown too. He said I should let Curtis Brown handle everything. He wrote a letter to Alan Collins, President of Curtis Brown, telling him, "You've got to take this man on." I forget the exact words, but he told him something like, "Fred is going to be a famous man someday." Alan read This is the Year and liked it.

Doubleday somehow got wind of the book. I guess they had their eye on me for a while. Ken McCormick, editor-in-chief, asked to have a copy over a weekend, at the same time Knopf got to their copy. George Shively, one of his editors, came in the next Monday morning and said, "We gotta have it." I was going to get a five hundred dollar advance from Webb; that's what we had talked about anyway. I got, I think, a $250 advance on the other two books. But Doubleday right away said $2500 for the advance. At least five times more than what Webb was going to offer me. Ten times more than I had received on the first two books.

Collins, however, said that he wasn't sure that I should go with Doubleday. He believed they wouldn't really know how to handle me, that I was more of a Knopf type author. I think he was dead right on that point. Doubleday never did learn how to merchandise my stuff. They merchandised me like I might be a sort of

Frank Slaughter popular kind of writer. Rather than present me to the considerate, intelligent reader that Knopf might have solicited.

We did get a letter later on from a Knopf editor about their copy of This Is The Year. He wanted me to completely rewrite it. He said I should write it so that it would look a little like Knut Hamsun's great novel, The Growth of the Soil. I wrote to Alan Collins and said the heck with that. Who is Hamsun? I'm Feike Feikema and I want it my way and Knut can have it his way. Why should I imitate that guy? I don't live in Norway. Hamsun picked his spot and got his ideas from that, from the Norway earth there, at that place. While I picked mine from around here. I designed my novel so that is looked like it came right out of the earth itself, here. I even used meteorological data. The substructure of This Is The Year is based on data for five years which I picked quite carefully. And I used that as the physical base for the book, the pillars on which I set the whole story. And couldn't destroy that. So that's how I landed with Doubleday.

Doubleday also took The Chokecherry Tree without any problems. They took it right away and loved it.

Then the same with The Primitive, The Brother, and The Giant. However, as we were going along, Doubleday became increasingly disenchanted with me. They didn't get the results they'd hoped they were going to get. The books received very good reviews except for the few pans The Brother got around New York. That's because the hero went to New York and he looked at it with Siouxland eyes and he didn't particularly care about New York. And you can't offend the gods in New York.

I made an error while writing those three though. I was into The Brother when I realized I should never have allowed The Primitive to get away until I'd had the whole trilogy finished. Ken McCormick had flown into Minneapolis and heard I had a trilogy underway. He said, "Why don't you let us have it book by book, and we'll print them, and then when we get them all done, we'll let you go through it again, clean it all up and then we'll do a final edition, like they did with Studs Lonigan." Thus, my original intent was to do the three in one book. In any case, Doubleday got quite disenchanted. They didn't make any money.

I next sent them a book called The Rape of Elizabeth. I also sent them another manuscript called The Mountain of Myrrh. Two different stories and Doubleday turned those down. I always felt Doubleday turned down The Rape of Elizabeth because Queen Elizabeth was in the news a lot at that point. I think that they felt a little uneasy about it, but I wasn't even thinking about the queen. I was very hard up too at that point in my life, so I put the two manuscripts on the back burner again. Then I got onto this tale called Lord Grizzly and I went real hard after that. A sub-editor at Random House went to Doubleday as sort of an intercessor for me. I had a sense of pride and I wasn't going to send them Lord Grizzly if they were going to turn it down. So he asked Doubleday if they'd do Grizzly and they said no. Well, at that point I asked for the rights all back to all my previous books there, which I eventually got.

It was at that time that I changed my name. In '52. Quite an upheaval was going on in my family. Two manuscripts had been turned down. We were broke, my wife was working part-time, and I was picking up what little work I could here and there. Pretty rough going. Our car didn't have lights so we couldn't go anywhere at night. But I had to write. While I was rewriting Lord Grizzly, I sent a rough copy to McGraw-Hill. Then I went off to Montana to check out a bunch of facts and details I wasn't sure about. While I was gone, McGraw-Hill sent a wire to my place saying, it's a great book, when can we have the final draft? My wife Maryanna got hold of me long distance, caught up with me at Fort Berthold. That query made me feel good. I knew that when I got home we'd clean up a few bills.

I rewrote the whole thing, made one more draft because I had picked up new material on the trip. Where the various forts were and so on.

I ran into one funny story. It happened on the scene where Hugh Glass finally catches up with young Jim Bridger, where the Little Big Horn and Yellowstone came together. I wanted to know where that fort was so I drove on a yard there. There was a lean guy hoeing out in a field. I walked over toward him. He stopped hoeing, and said, "What did I do now?" "Well, you didn't do anything wrong as far as I know, at least not yet," I said. We talked a little while, and then I said, "Why are you growing corn here? This isn't a place to plant corn. I'm from Iowa and we know where to plant corn. Grow it in black soil. This is awfully yellow clay." The guy said, "But you got to make a living somehow." I noticed a small area where the corn was growing tall and healthy. I asked him how come. It was about twice as tall as the other corn. As if there'd once been a manure pile there of some kind. "Oh," he said, "that's where General Custer screwed the chief's daughter and spilled it on the ground so he wouldn't get into trouble with his wife." That story tells you there's a myth at work there. It's about where Custer camped, above the Big Horn, before he got butchered.

Well, later, I looked at the two previously rejected manuscripts. I'm a damned stubborn Frisian. Once I've got something started, I hate to give up on it. I'd put too much in the two of them to just throw them away. I had set aside enough manuscripts in the past and I wasn't gonna give up any more of them. One evening I was talking to both my wife Maryanna and Russell Roth, the critic. Roth is a marvelously brilliant man, has a really fine mind. They were both listening to me talking about having to set the two manuscripts aside, muttering about them, <u>The Rape of Elizabeth</u> and <u>The Mountain of Myrrh</u>. What should I do with them? Both of them said at about the same time, "You know, Fred, all that work sounds like it's the same book. You're dealing with the same general problem in both books. They sound like they belong together." So that's what I did. I backed up and I went over the whole problem and that became <u>Morning Red</u>. That's why you have those alternating chapters in there. Towards the end they meld in together. I built it kind of like a tooth. A two-rooted tooth. Or, to make another metaphor, you can't bite into anything unless you got both the upper and lower set of teeth. And I do build books a little bit like that. That's the story of <u>Morning Red</u>.

<u>Morning Red</u> was maybe 800 pages in manuscript. I sent them all around New York. My honest guess would be that it was turned down some twenty times.

McGraw-Hill turned it down right off the bat. In fact, the editor-in-chief there, Ed Aswell, who was the second editor Thomas Wolfe had, provided me with a very interesting experience. Bartlett was my real man at McGraw-Hill, but Ed Aswell was his boss. And when I went in to see editor-in-chief Ed Aswell, I had the sensation that he gawked, almost gagged in his throat, when he saw me. Because suddenly there I was, bigger than Tom Wolfe. Tom Wolfe was his hero. I'd broken a precious image of his. Tom Wolfe was no longer the only literary Gargantua in the U.S.A. Well, Aswell also didn't like the theme of rape and all that in <u>Morning Red</u>. He told me to shelve it. I said I'd never do that,

that I'd get it printed somewhere. I said it was a masterpiece. I remember him kind of snickering and looking kind of funny at me, and he said, "Don't Tom Wolfe me." And I said, "Who's Tom Wolfe?"

Of course I knew who Tom Wolfe was, he was somebody that I couldn't read. I never liked him. I've only read maybe 80 - 90 pages of his. Maybe a 150, because I did read the essay he wrote about being tall. I forget the name of it. I tried to start his other books but I couldn't go on. He's too wordy and flowery for me. He didn't have that clear, sharp air to work in to get at things like we have here in our Siouxland atmosphere and our climate. Also we Frisians are quite precise; and, loaded with poetry.

Finally one day Herb Alexander at Pocketbooks said to me, "Why are you still sending that book around? Everybody knows Morning Red has been turned down everywhere. They know it's a rewritten version of the two books you sent around earlier that were also all turned down everywhere. You're just a damn fool sending it around."

Well, in the meantime I'd heard about Alan Swallow. I thought, I'll get an outside opinion on Morning Red. Take it out of New York and give it to someone who's maybe kind of against New York and see what he says. I wrote Swallow a note, and he said. "Fine, let me look at it." I drove over to his house in Denver with Maryanna, since I was going to do some research just then on Riders of Judgment anyway. I borrowed my brother Henry's Mercury. My old car, my old Ford, was falling apart. I gave Swallow the manuscript. Then we went on to Wyoming where I took photos as research material. Then we went home.

It was in December, 1955, when I received a long letter in the mail from Swallow. I started reading it coming back from the mailbox, and when I finally got near the house I had the whole thing read. It was three pages long, single-spaced. Maryanna was hanging out the clothes, when all of a sudden I started jumping up and down and flopping and rolling around on the ground, crying, "See, I was right! See, I was right!" She says, "You crazy nut, what's the matter with you, you got the fits?" I says, "Yeh, I got a great letter from Alan Swallow. He says Morning Red is a great book and he'd be happy to print it even though it's going to be hard on the pocketbook. He doesn't want to change a word in it." So that's how Morning Red got printed.

With Riders of Judgment Swallow told me to go to New York first to try to get it printed there.

Earlier, I had borrowed some money from the neighbors. And I got some money from Maryanna's mother, Gramma Shorba. I flew to New York and I stayed at The Players. Waring Jones was a friend of mine and I stayed at the club as his guest. (I'm now a member.) The first place I went to was the New York Times. I approached Harvey Breit, who wrote a column on books. He received me kindly and wondered what I wanted. I said, "I'd like to get some names from you, names of men you think are the best editors in town. Someone in the vein of Max Perkins. That's the kind of editor I've got to have. I can't handle the damn commercial editors. I've got to have somebody who understands what I'm up to." "Well," Harvey Breit said, "the two best in town are Roger Straus, Jr., and David McDowell." Then Harvey took me in to see Francis Brown, editor-in-chief. Francis took a liking to me. He asked me if I would send him an essay for their "Speaking of Books" column. Which I did, an article about Western literature. There were one or two others that I did for him.

That weekend I went to visit the guy who reviewed The Golden Bowl for the New York Sun. His name was Clayton Hoagland. His wife was Kathleen Hoagland, an Irish woman who edited a book called One Thousand Years of Irish Poetry. She also wrote a novel. As I was explaining my publishing problems to them, she says, "Why, David McDowell lives up the street here." It was Sunday morning by this time. (I'd arrived there Saturday afternoon.) So they called up David's house. David had been out on a toot the night before and had come in awful late. But when he heard that I was at the Hoaglands, he decided he should meet me. See, the curious thing is, I was one of those authors who had a good reputation, but no one wanted to take the risk of publishing me. Sort of a sub rosa reputation, you know, that I was a comer. A man with a good fast ball but who walked a lot of people. That's a pretty good description, ha. I probably was a little wild in their eyes, but I could really throw a hard ball.

David showered and shaved and refreshed himself with coffee and came over. We right away liked each other. I told him I was about to write a book called Riders of Judgment. I gave him a published copy of Lord Grizzly to read. A few days later he called me to say he liked Grizzly and very definitely would like to be my editor and work with me. He didn't care much for Morning Red. I let him read a copy of the original manuscript of that too. I think David perhaps reflected the scuttlebut that was going around New York about Morning Red; a reject novel, rewritten out of two novels. Those editors don't tell you anything. I have noticed several times that editors have to be politic, even when they are your friend. David liked Riders of Judgment when I delivered it, and that was how Random House took it. He was then at Random House.

All of a sudden he left Random House and set up a publishing house with Ivan Obolensky. David had the know-how and Ivan had the money. David took the rights of Riders of Judgment, shortly after it was published, over to the McDowell-Obolensky house with him. So, in other words, Riders of Judgment fell between two chairs. Nobody at Random House pushed it. So it just fell dead.

David next took Conquering Horse at his new house and there was no problem there. He liked the manuscript. It was the only place I submitted it.

Shortly after, David got into trouble with Ivan's lawyers, as I recall all this now. Ivan was actually working out of a trust fund and those trust fund lawyers thought David too powerful for Ivan. They were afraid that eventually the house would become the McDowell Publishing Company and Ivan would just vanish. So they pinched David out.

It almost broke David's heart. David had to scramble for a job for quite a while. It was funny and very sad. The New York publishing circles are not only terribly incestuous, they are one of the most gossip-ridden, small-time, penny-ante kind of people you ever saw in your life. They have this big pretense to intellectuality, and they are all very intellectual, but I've noticed that when intellectuals gossip, they're ten times worse than the average guy from Doon, Iowa. The effect of it is more powerful. The average guy can't do more than stir up a little fuss. David finally ran the Kraus Imprints for awhile. Kraus Imprints reprinted almost all of the little magazines ever printed in America.

I had to find a new publisher. It took awhile. Meanwhile, Alan Swallow wanted to do more for me, and when earlier I couldn't get Random House to take a collection of short stories I had, just before I followed David to McDowell, Obolensky, I sent them to Swallow. Swallow said he liked the three novelettes in the collection. We called them Arrow of Love and he did those.

He was also after me to rewrite the Trilogy, which I'd already begun to do. I said earlier that when I was in the second volume, I realized I should never have let The Primitive get away until the whole trilogy was done. For one thing, I couldn't change names. Caught by the errors in the first volume, you have to stick by them in the second one. And in the third volume you're caught by the errors you made in the first and second. Yes, I really should have waited until the whole thing was done and then corrected it all in one straight version. So that's what I did next. I literally took the bound copies, cut the work on the printed page, and then retyped it as I went along. Those three copies by the way are in the University of Minnesota Library Archives. They're all marked up. I rewrote some sections, cut some, changed names in the new version. I had over-Frisianized names in the first Primitive copy. It's smoother now. Wanderlust to me is the way it should be. I wish all the prior copies could be retrieved so that I could burn them. But there are too many out there. Only 500 copies of Wanderlust were actually bound. There were more loose sheets. The new Swallow people, the Chicago people who bought out Alan's estate after he died, never bound them. I don't know what happened to them.

Then I wrote Scarlet Plume. My agent sent that around. I don't actually know how many rejections the agent got. Every once in awhile he's send me a resume. I once figured out there were at least 20 rejections. One day it landed with Herb Alexander's outfit, Trident Press. Trident Press was the hardcover side of Pocketbooks, owned by Simon & Schuster. He had just hired an editor named Bucklin Moon. Buck had been at Doubleday when I was there. Buck had always wished that he'd had me, instead of George Shively's being my editor. Buck was a first-rate editor. He'd found J.F. Powers' Prince of Darkness, for example. Scarlet Plume landed on his desk. He read it and liked it. Within a few weeks we had a contract signed.

Later a curious thing happened there. Some months after Plume was published, it all of a sudden started to take off. There were four printings in about a space of three or four weeks. The publicity director, Andrew Ettinger, called me about it a couple of times, said he was urging Herb to really put the big push behind it. But Herb finally decided that, since Trident Press was a subsidiary of Simon and Schuster, he had to be careful with what he did with their money. Herb's a hard-nosed guy. Very bright, but hard-nosed. So he preferred to put their promotion money, the big push, into Harold Robbins' new book instead of mine, and that's how that happened.

I next sent in The Man Who Looked Like the Prince of Wales. I had been meaning to start King of Spades, but then instead I got this bright idea. I heard a friend of mine had died. I felt terrible about that. I really loved that man and I wanted to do a memorial as a remembrance. He was a man who had had some really tough luck with two different women. And he got the dickens from the Church. Everybody pointed fingers at him. Had he been in my profession today, he would have been known as a rather wonderful macho Hemingway kind of guy. He was bright and quick and a good athlete. But that extra brain that wasn't being used had to be satisfied in some way so he took to drink. I wrote the first draft of that story in about three weeks while I was at the Huntington Hartford Foundation. Later, when I got home, I polished it. About then, Buck Moon wrote to ask if I had another book. Yes, I said, I have this little thing. He said, send it to me. He read it, said it was a good book, that it probably would be a good seller. He kept my working title, The Man Who Looked Like the Prince of Wales, the only title I could think of. Later on, it came out as The Secret Place in the paperback version.

Winter Count never went anywhere but to James Theuson, a publisher in Minneapolis. He had heard I had a collection of poems and asked me if he couldn't see it. He was one of those fellows who had a full-time job, but liked to fancy himself a publisher of special books. He's now a librarian at the Minnesota Historical Society. Winter Count later was reprinted by Paul Foreman of Thorp Springs Press, Austin, Texas.

Buck Moon instantly liked King of Spades. And it is a deep book. The other day I was looking through King of Spades so I could write an introductory essay for it for the G. K. Hall Gregg Press reprints of The Buckskin Man Tales. Well, I just can't write essays. That's a foreign way of doing things for me. I'm an evoker and a story-teller and a from-the-roots-up kind of a guy. In an essay you've got to come in from the top and then crush it together in order to find something there. I've been at it two weeks now and I've only got five pages here. It's driving me wild. I'm to explain why I wrote King of Spades.

Many people don't understand why I wrote it. They think I was just bringing in, importing, the Oedipus complex. The truth is, I stumbled onto the idea for the book. I ran into a good story in a local paper and I got intrigued in it; and then I thought, when I was pretty well along in it, hey, that's right, two other guys have been here, Sophocles and Shakespeare. Well, too bad for them. So I went ahead anyway. There are some great things in _King of Spades_, especially that passage where Ransom meets Erden Aldridge. I'll never beat that writing. Every paragraph jumps at you like a poem. I was home alone part of that summer; my wife was gone on a trip. Just Freddie was with me, but I didn't see much of him except at supper. He was out playing baseball and riding his bicycle and running around over the Blue Mounds. So all day long I had that wonderful high home up there on the Blue Mounds all by myself. I just exploded.

Trident liked _Apples of Paradise_ right away too. You remember I had that collection of short stories from which I pulled the three novelettes, _Arrow of Love_? The remainder became a book called _Apples of Paradise_. Both of those books, _Arrow of Love_ and _Apples of Paradise_, in effect were turned down by Random House. But Buck Moon liked _Apples of Paradise_. He told me they had to be printed.

Same way with _Eden Prairie_. That just went over with a real bang with Buck. We just had no trouble at all. Trident wanted it.

And then _Conversations_. I did those television tapes in '64 at the University of South Dakota. I had met an editor, Trudy McMurrin, from the University of Utah Press and she asked me if they couldn't print something of mine. I told her about those tapes John R. Milton had had transcribed in rough for me. She said, why don't you edit them? I had to go and listen to some of the audio part of the tapes to redo the transcription. I could hardly stand to do it. I don't like going over old stuff. Later, one of the readers for the University of Utah Press wasn't sure he liked it. He said, "Well, I read the whole thing and I still don't know how to write a novel."

Then I wrote _Milk of Wolves_ and was busy with that for a couple of years. At the time I thought I was writing the greatest American novel ever written. So I sent that East, to Trident Press. Buck Moon had left them by that time. Herb Alexander sent it back to me. He made the literary excuse that it wasn't really a very good book. Part of the excuse, as I recall it now, was that Trident had tried five books of mine now and they'd had no luck with me, so maybe it was time to part company. So then we tried it everywhere. My agent finally gave up on it. Then I personally sent it around for awhile. Altogether that novel had at least 20, I'd almost guess 30 rejections. I was terribly disheartened.

I thought, you know, my goodness, here I think that I've written my best book and they think it's the worst. What's wrong with me? What's wrong with my judgment? What's wrong with my antennae, what's wrong with my lizard, my interior commentator? You know, it really shook me up. It kind of ticked me off, what was going on. First Herb Alexander said no. And then soon it was all over New York that Fred'd written another book like Morning Red.

One editor, who shall remain nameless, read the manuscript of Milk of Wolves and was considerably upset by it. He called me long distance in the evening, telling the operator to charge the call to his business number. "Fred, what I'm going to have to tell you is going to be the most difficult decision I've ever had to make. We can't publish it. I'm sorry to tell you this because it has in it some of the best writing you've ever done. But, you know, the basic premise of the book is wrong. You know artists are not like that. Artists are sensitive, even delicate, people, very understanding souls, like you yourself are, and they'd never do what this Juhl Melander of yours does in Milk of Wolves, screwing all those women models of his, and all the neighbor women. Artists aren't like that at all. They are wonderful people, gentle, and if they do occasionally stray, it's not done brutally like your Juhl does it." The editor'd had a couple of drinks, and it doesn't pay to argue with one who is, so to speak, ahead of you with the alcohol.

But I did object a little. I told him that it was my book and my notion about the artist and he really had no right to tell me how to think. It was my experience, I said, that some artists were exactly like Juhl. I'd known some like him. And they had a right to representation in novels, and in particular, in my novels. But he still said, no, he could not publish it. Later on I found out that he privately had fought to have it published with his house but that he had been overruled.

As we talked he mentioned one writer, William Carlos Williams, who he thought was one of those tender and considerate artists. That almost made me laugh. Because I'd heard the tale that after Bill Williams had had his first stroke, he'd confessed to his wife Flossie that he'd slept with some of the women they knew. After that Flossie practically kept poor old Bill locked up.

Now, in the meantime a man named Neill McCaffrey, a gallant kind of fellow who'd once had a prominent position in Washington, one day called me long-distance. And then later on visited me. His wife had just divorced him and his life was all broken up. To get back into the swim of things, he had to go for a big killing. He'd fallen in love with Conquering Horse and wanted to make a movie out of it. I told him Michael Cimino already had an option on it. Neill's son Vince, just out of Harvard, had also read Conquering Horse. That book woke Vince up to who I was. Vince owned a bookstore and wanted to become an editor someday. He started reading my books and finally wrote me to ask if he couldn't print one of my books. Well, I jumped for that and sent him Milk of Wolves. He fell in love with it, said it was my best book. So he went into hock to print that. His girl friend Thais helped him. They borrowed the rest from a friend.

Now we're talking about 1970, somewhere in there, when I started writing Green Earth. I finally decided it was time to do that one. I'd put enough distance between me and that early life of mine. And of course my father and mother. I'd also just picked up some information from my Uncle Hank about my mother. Mother'd had another boyfriend before my father, something I hadn't known. I looked the guy up in the guise of someone who could help him. He lived in Maurice, Iowa. I wanted to see what kind of a guy my mother might be interested in. He turned out to be a handsome man, like my father, tall and lean. Black hair, bright eyes, like my father had. I also thought that at the age of 58 I'd have enough distance from those early days so that I could make the book read somewhat like a classic.

It took me quite a few years to write. I wrote in longhand. From Lord Grizzly on I wrote all my books in longhand, first draft. Before that I wrote them on the typewriter. I wrote Green Earth in big green ledgers. I think it was 13.

As I started to type it up, I ran across a friend I'd once known for years up in Minneapolis. William Lemons. He and I liked to talk about Indians. He'd once lived with them at the Standing Rock Reservation. It was Lemons who'd introduced me to Angela Fiske, a full-blooded Yankton Dakota, who became my chief informant for Conquering Horse. One day at the University of South Dakota, where we were both in the English Department, Bill handed me some pages he'd xeroxed from Lavender's Dent's Fort about a boy named Flat Warclub. It was kind of a nice story. Some time went by and then he gave me another little xeroxed account about a society of Indian women. The Crow Indian women had a kind of a club they called The Manly Hearted

Women. On the way home from teaching my class that day, it all of a sudden hit me -- what would have happened had Flat Warclub ever run into a Manly Hearted Woman? By the time I got home I had it all outlined on a clipboard. I usually have a clipboard with me in the car. So the next day I dropped work on Green Earth and I started writing The Manly-Hearted Woman. That was in June. It took just a couple of months that summer to write the first draft. Later that winter I read that first draft; decided it was good; and again interrupted the final typing of Green Earth to make a final draft of The Manly-Hearted Woman. My agent sent it first to Harcourt, Brace, Jovanovich. They read it and said no. Then another guy at Dell, William Decker, a former cowboy, who'd wanted to meet me, read it and decided he couldn't do it. And then, it went to David McDowell, who was back in the business at Crown. David liked it right off. No problem.

Through with Manly-Hearted Woman, I went back to Green Earth, finished typing it up, then I put it away because I didn't quite know what to do with it. I knew it was too long, 1607 pages of manuscript.

Then we had the big explosion. We had to leave our home up on the Blue Mounds. It was terrible, terrible. The upshot was finally that I had to buy these few acres of land, Roundwind, start this garden, dig this hole for a new house here, haul my old writing cabin over here, the one we're sitting in now, which I'd taken along with me from Bloomington in 1960. In the meantime I gave my wife such money as we got from the sale of the other place to the State of Minnesota. And we separated. She moved to Sioux Falls. I had little or no money. I was really strapped.

At first, though, when we were still up on the Blue Mounds, we all thought of resisting the eviction. Just not go. But, Vander Kooi, my lawyer, told me that if we persisted, the State could get us for illegal trespass on state property. It would go on our record. "You're living on someone's property illegally."

During the time we were thinking of resisting the state, I'd had a wonderful idea. I'd heard that during the last war the government wanted to flush the Hutterites off their land in South Dakota. But the head man of the Hutterites out-maneuvered the government. He told all the Hutterite women to undress and lie stark naked on the floor. Their women usually wore long black dresses. When the federal marshalls arrived, they found all these naked women on the floor. Well, seeing that, they backed off and left them alone. So, I thought to myself, that's what I'm going to do when the sheriff comes. I'm going to take off all my clothes and lie on the floor. My two daughters thought that a great idea too. "Dad, we'll join you." And son Freddie said, "Yeh, you bet." Maryanna laughed and said she'd just sit there and watch us.

Meanwhile, I was being called up by all kinds of radio and television people, "What's going on over there?" Each time I told them "Nothing." I told the state boys, though, that I could give them a lot of bad publicity, that I was holding the media off. But they thought I was just bluffing. Lawyer Vander Kooi told them I wasn't, that we were all set to do the television scene if they came to haul us off. The whole works would be there when the sheriff started hauling us out of there naked.

Finally, I decided we should just move off, and that I'd fight alone for damages. The state had once promised me life estate, that we could live there until I died. I went to the Department of Administration to present our case. I went to hearings and hearings. Then at the last hearing, the one before a legislative committee, I spoke first, then the lawyer for the Department of Natural Resources presented their side of it, then I asked if I could question the lawyer. I made several points. He didn't question me. Nor did the committee question me, but they did question him, gave him a grilling. I had my argument all memorized. No papers to shuffle, everything terse, no BS, no fat, absolutely skin, bones, and muscle. I spoke for about five minutes. Bang. That's all. Finally they voted unanimously to give me the extra money I asked for. So that's out of our hair now. But that was a wild time, and I didn't get much done.

Meanwhile, David McDowell learned that I had this big long book in my files. He asked if they couldn't look at it. I said, "Well, I should read it over first." "Let us look at it," he said, "and we can tell you what we think of it, and then you can have a final go at it." So I sent a copy to him and to Herb Michelman in April, 1976.

I didn't hear from him or from Herb at Crown for weeks and weeks. Then one day about the middle of September the phone rang and there was David McDowell. He asked how I was and what the weather was like. Finally he said, "Well, I read your novella." I knew two things right away. First, he liked it. Second, it was too long. "What's wrong with it?" "Well, it's obviously a book you wrote over many years. And it's obvious too that you took notes on this for many years." It was true. The very first note I ever took in my life for a book was on Green Earth, when I was at Calvin. I was lonesome for my mother. I wrote notes, memory notes, about my mother, in the back of my leather notebook. And that became the germ of Green Earth. Took that long to germinate. McDowell went on to say that I often forgot that I'd already introduced various characters. "We already know who they are, yet you keep introducing them. It's repetitious." I right away knew what he meant. "You're too close to it," David said, "and it took too long to do it. So you forgot what you had down. So why don't you fly in and we'll go over it together."

David and Herb Michelman both agreed that even as it stood it was a great book and reminded them a lot of Thomas Wolfe, except that the style was more clear, more readable, and as a book, better organized. I came home. I made it the rule to cut at least two lines each page. But you know, I wound up cutting eight-plus lines a page. I usually average about 24 lines a page. So I cut it more than a third, almost two-fifths. And then I sent it in.

They read the book again and I once more had to go back because David found several things that still weren't right. One passage I decided would hurt certain people and I removed it. But I left in a notation in my will that when everybody is dead the scene can be replaced. I wanted it in there. It makes Free more mortal. It detracts a little from him. And I want to keep that picture whole. Not load it too much in his favor.

Crown looked at The Wind Blows Free. Herb Michelman held it a long, long time. Finally Herb told me that he liked it, but he'd like for me to set it aside for awhile and instead he'd like to do my next novel. I made the mistake of telling him I was on a long novel. I said I like to have the books printed in the order that I wrote them. Not confuse people. Nor confuse me either. No, he wanted it set aside. I asked if I could send it to the Center for the Western Studies at Augustana College in Sioux Falls. They'd heard about it and they'd like to do one book of mine. Crown said, all right, but if they turn it down, you've got to send it back to us. So that's what I did. The center for Western Studies took one look at it and said they'd like to do it. So that's the story on The Wind Blows Free. I'm still with Crown and they're now reading Sons of Adam.*

*Published September, 1980.

Postscript

An author's publishing career is in many respects related to public recognition. Two of Manfred's novels have been in final competition for major literary awards: <u>This is the Year</u> for the Pulitzer Prize and <u>Lord Grizzly</u> for the <u>National Book</u> Award. The following comments are excerpted from a talk by Manfred entitled "Usable Wests," and delivered on October 28, 1980, at the University of South Dakota. The comments here are edited from a transcript of a tape recording of the address. The address has been published in full in the <u>South Dakota Review</u>, XVIII (Winter, 1981), pp. 64-80 under the title "Usable Wests".

* * * * * * * * * * *

Can I tell you two stories that just might be true? They're usable. The first one is about <u>This Is The Year</u>, my third book. By that time I was really starting to take off as a novelist. Instead of pitching, say, a nine-hitter and winning 3-2 in <u>The Golden Bowl</u>, and pitching a seven-hitter and winning 2-1 in <u>Boy Almighty</u>, I was now going for a no-hitter and winning 1-0 in <u>This Is The Year</u>. And I did pretty well in that book too. It got good reviews, went for two editions. It was published in the spring of 1947, and at the end of the year the Associated Press held a roundup of all book editors in America asking them to nominate the best novel of the year. Ken McCormick, my editor-in-chief at Doubleday, sent me a copy of an AP wire release, announcing <u>This Is The Year</u> as the near unanimous choice.

About three months later my wife and I went to Robert Penn Warren's house for dinner. Red greeted us at the door, gentleman that he was. He looked at me with a whimsical smile, wet his finger, and said, "Let me touch you." I said, "What's going on here?" "Well," he said, "the word is you're going to get the Pulitzer in May." (Warren had won it the May before for his novel <u>All The King's Men</u>.) Well, I'd had a lot of hard knocks in my life by that time, had lost several real 1-0 baseball games, so I wasn't about to have any sleepless nights over it. I didn't say very much. Thus when I didn't get it in May, I wasn't too disappointed.

The next story involves my Lord Grizzly, published in 1954. That was the year that William Faulkner's A Fable came out. Rough competition. A few months before the National Book Awards were to be announced, Red Warren wrote me a card, just as he and his family were leaving for Italy, saying he liked Lord Grizzly and was voting for it in the NBA derby. Lord Grizzly and A Fable were two of the five novels nominated in the fiction category. There were three judges and Red Warren was one of them. The judges were to vote five for first place, three for second, and one for third. As it turned out, Faulkner, who'd never won an NBA award, got it for his A Fable.

So I lost out on that one too. That one would have been nice to have had, to beat out Faulkner. However, I didn't weep over it very long. I was already busy writing a new book when the award was announced.